The Teacher Book
Finding Personal and Professional Balance

Bobbi Fisher

D0850996

HEINEMANN
Portsmouth, NH

Heinemann
A division of Reed Elsevier Inc.
361 Hanover Street
Portsmouth, NH 03801–3912
www.heinemann.com

Offices and agents throughout the world

Library of Congress Cataloging-in-Publication Data
Fisher, Bobbi.
    The teacher book : finding personal and professional balance / Bobbi Fisher.
        p.   cm.
    Includes bibliographical references.
    ISBN 0-325-00314-9 (pbk : alk. paper)
    1. Teachers—United States—Attitudes.   2. Teachers—Professional relationships—United States.   I. Title.

LB1775.2 .F59 2000
371.1—dc21

                                                    00-040962

Editor: Lois Bridges
Production coordinator: Vicki Kasabian
Production service: Melissa L. Inglis
Cover design: Jenny Jensen Greenleaf
Manufacturing: Deanna Richardson

Printed in the United States of America on acid-free paper
04   03   02   01   00   DA   1   2   3   4   5

This book is dedicated to classroom teachers.

CONTENTS

ACKNOWLEDGMENTS

THERE WAS never any question. Of course I would dedicate this book to classroom teachers. Thank you for writing this book with me. You have the most honorable job in the world. I consider you my friends.

Other friends have also supported me in writing this book:

My personal friends, Jeanne Cole, Debby Cornwell, Mary Kurth, and Edie Murray.

My friends at Memorial Congregational Church, who have continued to help me balance my personal and professional life and stay centered, my teaching parish committee and my minister, Reverend Lisa Schoenwetter.

My e-mail teacher friends, Marilyn Carpenter, Sarah Cresswell, Mary Glover, Don Graves, and Ellen Silverman, who have listened, questioned, challenged, and sent positive energy.

My friends at Andover Newton Theological School: Julieanne Hallman, who was willing to support my alternative field education project, which included learning about spiritual direction on the Internet with teachers and writing this book; Professor Bob Pazmino, who provided inspiring feedback on the early stages of the manuscript; and my fellow students, who are walking the journey with me; my friend and field education advisor, Fran Bogle, who has encouraged me to find the sacred and the holy in what I write.

"The Group," my nine teacher friends throughout the country who have participated in my field education project.

My friends at Heinemann, especially Lois Bridges, Melissa Inglis, Leigh Peake, and Susie Stroud, for encouraging this project, and Ray Coutu, who got this project underway.

And finally, but most important, my closest friends: my family, who are an essential part of the balance; my mother; my husband, Jim; my son, Tim, his wife, Carin, and their daughter, Jemma, who was born in 1999; my daughter, Emily, her husband, Stephen, and their son, Colin, born in 1998; and my sisters, Alice and Margot, and my brother, Ross, and their families.

INTRODUCTION

In 1994, I took a leave of absence from classroom teaching. I was finishing up the final draft of *Thinking and Learning Together* and The Wright Group had just completed the filming for *Classroom Close-ups,* a videotape series of my first-grade classroom. I wanted to devote more time to giving workshops about classroom practice, and I knew I couldn't do that successfully while teaching full-time.

As I began this new work, teachers around the country told me about their love of teaching *and* the stresses that went along with the job as they tried to balance their personal and professional lives. I remembered the stresses during my teaching days, and how difficult it was at times to stay centered and balanced. I also remembered how, as a teacher, I was expected to "do it all" with a smile and that there were few public forums to discuss these issues. About that time I began thinking about writing a book to address these concerns, and started giving workshops and talks about ways we can balance our personal and professional lives.

In February 1999, I sent an e-mail letter to about twenty-five teacher friends, explaining this publishing project, asking some specific questions, and requesting that they e-mail the letter to interested colleagues. The response was overwhelming, and I began receiving e-mail from all over the country. My letter was put on the CATENet listserv (California Association of Teachers of English) and Teachers.Net (The Online Resource for Educators). I answered each e-mail, and developed an ongoing correspondence with many of the teachers. As my letter spread throughout cyberspace and I heard from more and more teachers, I sent out summary letters and asked other questions that were generated from the responses (see the Appendix).

Altogether, I heard from more than two hundred individual teachers from forty-five states, as well as teachers from Canada and one from Ecuador. The majority were kindergarten and first-grade teachers, but I also received e-mail from preschool, elementary, middle school, and high school teachers, as well as curriculum coordinators and teacher educators. I received more e-mail from California than any other state. These teachers in particular voiced the stresses that standards and testing have placed on them and their students. Many teachers expressed gratitude that I was there to listen to their concerns, and were hopeful that their voices might be heard.

The first section of this book is mostly written in the words of teachers who wrote to me about how they continually work to balance their intense professional lives with their busy personal lives, which include their immediate families, their aging parents, church and civic responsibilities, the need to maintain their health, their pursuit of a hobby or interest, and their longing to find personal fulfillment in relationships. Their responses are both universal and specific. Almost all the teachers mention that they find joy when a child learns, and most said that they stay in teaching because they are committed to making the world a better place. Although their classroom situations and personal lives vary greatly, most wrote that excessive testing, and non-teaching duties, such as meetings and paperwork, diminish both the quality of their teaching and the depth of children's learning.

The second section of the book explores some of the strategies for balancing our personal and professional lives that I have developed from my experiences dealing with stress and striving for balance in my own life and have shared with teachers in talks and workshops. I have discovered that the better I know myself, the more successful I am in becoming and staying centered, and I have found that teachers in my workshops are able to apply and adapt these strategies to their own situations and discover their unique formulas for staying centered. These strategies include (1) clarifying our present situation, (2) using the joys of childhood play and our own literacy experiences as mirrors for discovering our interests and attitudes, (3) naming principals of living, or what I call nuggets of truth, and exploring our own spirituality, and (4) taking action by writing mission statements and taking time for ourselves. Throughout this section, I have provided reflection questions for those of you who wish to spend more time considering your own situation. You may want to use a personal journal to help you respond these questions.

1

Centering and Balancing

I think the whole balancing act is the hardest thing, especially trying to get a meal on the table at the end of the day when the entire
family is wiped out and then staying up and planning for tomorrow's classes.

High school math teacher, Minnesota

WHEN I was a classroom teacher, there were many days when I was
surrounded by worries and didn't feel very centered or that my life was
in balance. Some of my worries were self-initiated: Was I paying
enough attention to handwriting? Was my class quiet enough in the
lunch line? Should I change the bulletin board in the hall more often?
Other worries involved issues of the profession: Was I meeting the individual needs of my students? Was I communicating honestly and
positively with parents? Was I addressing curriculum rigorously
enough? As the years went by, political issues relating to schools began
to affect my teaching world, such as systematic phonics versus whole
language, basal texts versus trade books, spelling tests versus invented
spelling, and standardized tests versus authentic student and teacher
accountability. In the midst of all this, I had responsibilities and commitments to my family, friends, and community. In order to function
competently, it was important that I address these educational issues
and develop strategies to overcome my worries.

Through in-person and e-mail conversations, I have discovered
that many teachers have concerns similar to mine, and that these

concerns are escalating as the number of challenges in education increases. Every day, teachers encounter children who come to school hungry, homeless, and feeling unsafe; parents who either want special attention for their child or who do not support their child's education; large class sizes; special needs children with no adult classroom assistance; an increasingly growing schoolwide curriculum with few resources and no time in the day to implement it; and the pressures of standardized testing. Teachers have complex lives outside of school, as well.

Centering and *balancing* are the two words I use in this book to describe the state of mind and condition of living that can help us be better teachers in our professional lives and better family members, friends, and citizens in our personal lives. When I mention these words to teachers, they say, "Yes, I want to be centered. Oh, I desperately need balance in my life." We ask ourselves: Am I centered? What do I need to do in this situation to get centered? How can I center that child? Why do I feel out of balance? What must I do to restore peace, joy, and balance in my life?

What does being centered and balanced mean? To me, being centered is feeling internally peaceful regardless of the circumstances, and that being balanced is feeling that I am addressing all the daily events of my life in the "right" proportions.

Centering

In this book, centering and balancing are related but not synonymous concepts. Joan Borysenko, biologist, psychologist, and writer on spirituality, claims that there is a difference between our inner balance and outer balance. I suggest that centering refers to our inner balance, and that the way we balance our personal and professional lives encompasses our outer balance.

Centering is an overall state of mind that includes a spiritual stance in our personal and professional lives, whereas balancing involves the details and events of living. To be centered is a state of mind in which I can accept and work through stressful situations and appreciate and value joyful ones. To use the words of Parker Palmer, teacher and writer on issues of education, community, spirituality, and social change, when I am centered I reveal "the inner landscape of the teaching self," which includes my "intellectual, emotional, and spiritual" self (Palmer 1998, 4).

For some, centering work may encompass a particular religious discipline, while for others it may invoke a more general quest for peace and calmness. When we take on the work of centering, we begin to respond to whatever happens to us as an opportunity to strive for joy, peace, and balance and to accept the gifts that we have been given. Centering can be a key word to remind us to keep peaceful as we move through the day: one of our pupils comes in crying—*help him to center;* the art teacher is absent and there is no sub—*keep centered;* it's raining and the class can't get out to play—*better center them;* a parent wants a conference every week—*get centered;* our own children miss the bus—*stay centered;* we have to carpool to three soccer games in one afternoon—*be centered.* When we are centered, it is easier for us to respond positively. Our emotional and cognitive lives are ordered and integrated.

When I talk about centering, I often put my fingertips together and, in contact with my body, move my hand from in front of my forehead to my heart, where it rests. For me, centering is about the heart. On the other hand, when I talk about balance, I place both hands, palms up and out from my body, and move them up and down as in a balance scale. My hands are in space, responding to the universe. For me, balance involves living with others at a particular time and place.

To me, centering is a prerequisite to being balanced. The more centered I am, the more my life is in balance. When I asked teachers, "Does being centered and being balanced mean the same to you?" most said the two concepts weren't the same but were connected. Teachers went onto say that if they weren't somewhat centered, it would be difficult for them to be balanced. Having balance in their lives enhanced the possibility of being centered. Listen to them express this in their own words.

> I think that balance and centering are distinctly different but interrelated, in that when I am living my life in a balanced way, I am also usually pretty centered.
>
> *Fourth-grade teacher, Oregon*

> In my mind, they are not the same. But, I don't think they're mutually inclusive or exclusive of each other and probably the people

3

who are most successful, both in the eyes of others and in their personal estimation, have both.

Kindergarten teacher, Nebraska

Not quite, but the two are so intertwined that it would be easy to see them as the same thing. Being balanced increases the likelihood that you will be centered, and being centered gives you the mental space to monitor the balance in your life.

Elementary curriculum specialist, California

For me being centered and balanced are, I think, a lot alike. Being centered is being focused, having priorities in order. I'm calm, but also energized because I'm not spending too much time in one area or another.

Staff developer, California

In responding to the question, "What does being centered mean to you and how do you know when you are centered?" some teachers identified it with their own values and commitment.

Centering is being grounded in your values and knowing who you truly are.

First-grade teacher, Oregon

Centered to my way of thinking is having convictions, being comfortable with those convictions and content with the way you are pursuing the goals of those convictions. The 3 Cs here seem to me to be synonymous with being well-grounded and goal-oriented, an idea of where you are headed.

Kindergarten teacher, Nebraska

Others felt that being centered includes some connection with a higher being, and some said that their religious faith centered them.

To me it means being in a place where you know that you are not the one in control or solely responsible, that there are colleagues and a higher power all involved and all doing their parts. This brings about a perspective on all situations, a calmness, and thus an ability to see the beautiful things all around you.

Curriculum specialist, California

I think that being centered means being focused and clear. When I am centered I have a clear understanding of my abilities, my limits and my goals. I think that being centered is the antithesis of being egotistical because when I am centered I am not at all aware of the impression I am making or my reputation with the people around me. In my spiritual life I am most centered when I feel that the Spirit of Christ is living in me and through me.

Fourth-grade teacher, Oregon

Balance

To me, being balanced means that whatever is going on in my life is getting the attention I feel it needs. At certain times in my life it was easy to stay centered and my life seemed very balanced. But, when my children were little, my balance was teetery, and shifting from day to day. I had to work hard to maintain daily equilibrium as I transported my daughter to day care, did the grocery shopping, cooked meals, played games with and read to my children, spent time with my husband, while at the same time I planned for and taught kindergarten, communicated with parents, attended meetings, and kept up with professional readings. Many of my personal interests and friendships got put on the back burner. When my children went off to college, my life was easier to balance. I could think in terms of days, weeks, and months, instead of hours.

Being balanced means different things to different people, as shown in the following responses to the question, "What does being balanced mean to you, and how do you know when you are balanced?"

I think the concept of balance is so personal. You could look at someone else's life and declare them unbalanced, when it is just right for them!

Kindergarten teacher, Nebraska

When I'm balanced there is an evenness between my work and personal life—when I feel that I'm devoting the right amount of time to each, and not saying, "Family is more important," and then spending all my time at work!

First-grade teacher, Oregon

Balance is about successfully juggling the most important values in my life. For me these are my work, my family, my Christianity, and myself. I feel most like my life is balanced when I am paying attention to all of these areas in my life and one area is not monopolizing my time.

Fourth-grade teacher, Oregon

I love to share new books with kids so I buy several. Do you think maybe buying books helps us stay balanced? That would make me feel less guilty about the big stack I bought yesterday!??! It is one of my favorite parts of teaching!

Third-grade teacher, Ohio

Many teachers feel comfortable with the balance tipped unequally for a while as long as they know that the weights will change. During the school year, the professional side of my scale often got very heavy. But during vacations, the personal balance took over, especially when we went away from home for a vacation.

Being balanced seems just what it says, that there is an equilibrium in the balance among personal, professional, and familial demands. It's not necessarily equal time, but sufficient time for each with occasional "makeups" of time for any neglected facet of life. The work with standards in my district has run into evenings, so now my gardening time on weekends is more critical than the housework, and I'll catch up on the housework later, or actually break down and get some housekeeping help now and then to keep the balance. The alternative would be to nag family members, grouse about working too hard, etc. Of course, being broke makes it hard to find alternatives and you fall into feeling trapped.

First-grade teacher, Oregon

A teacher from Nebraska uses the image of a pie to describe the multiple roles she plays in the variety of events in her life. She suggests that we get stressed when there are more pieces than can fit on the plate, or when we focus too much on one piece. At first I thought about balanced in the context of a balance scale, but I think it is much more complex than that—it is more like a flexible pie chart.

> Some people may balance their life with multiple segments while others focus on two or three. At different times in your life some segments may increase or decrease. With the "empty nest" stage I am in right now, the children section has decreased in daily need but I hope it will enlarge again one day with grandchildren needs! A young parent may have mostly family and job with tiny segments for volunteer, religion, and hobbies. At certain times of the year, my "pie chart" flexes such as a major growth in the volunteer section the month or so before state conference!! That's when household chores and quality spouse time diminish to equalize the circle! If you feel jostled, hassled, and frazzled, you're not balanced. You must have more than 100 percent on your graph! It is also possible that one's fixation on a single piece to the neglect of the other is the first clue that things are out of balance.
>
> *Kindergarten teacher, Nebraska*

I e-mailed back:

> Your image of the pie is very clear and descriptive. Of course sometimes, especially with pizza, we try to take the biggest piece and then get sick. That's when we are out of balance. Pieces do change size, depending on how we cut them. I guess we are best when we have the knife in hand, rather than give it over to others (administrators, family). I'd like to come up with a different metaphor than knife, with its sharp edge, cutting being permanent, no softness. Perhaps a spatula. I also like your idea about how the pie changes at different times of the year, and in the life cycle. Thanks for your thoughts.

Another teacher also used the image of a pie as she explained that sometimes she is balanced when she has a lot going on, and at other times is overwhelmed by all that is happening in her life.

I know I can either be balanced with a variety of tasks or be over-whelmed. Having a finger in every pie, or should I say every finger in a different pie (which always seems to be the case) leaves me impatient and quick-tempered. To an observer, my busy life may seem in balance but it can definitely be "out of whack"!

First-grade teacher, California

I responded that sometimes I, too, put all my fingers in many pies, and that when no one is looking, I put my toes in as well.

Parker Palmer writes, "But a good teacher must stand where the personal and public meet, dealing with the thundering flow of traffic at an intersection where 'weaving a web of connectedness' feels more like crossing a freeway on foot" (1998, 17). The voices of teachers heard in this book tell of the many ways that they work to center themselves and to achieve balance in their personal and professional lives in order to successfully deal with the "thundering freeways" they face each day.

2

The Joys of Teaching

It's the kids who keep me centered.

High school English teacher, California

I absolutely love teaching anyone anything, and that in itself brings me great joy. I also just flat out love kids, and teaching them brings me huge delight. I love working with struggling readers, and helping them gain tools that enable them to be successful, and feel like readers. I also love working with tough kids, and helping them learn to manage themselves. I feel the most joy, I think, when I redeem a kid, or help a kid find himself.

Staff developer, Colorado

Teaching is a tonic for what ails ya. It's very hard work, as you well know, but it's so wonderfully rewarding, such joyful work, that it turns your sorrows into dancing. You may go to work with grief or pain, and then come home happy, or at least happier, at least most of the time.

Kindergarten teacher, Oregon

WITHOUT EXCEPTION, every teacher who e-mailed me in response to the question, "What are the times you feel joy in your teaching?" said that it was seeing their students learn that gave them the greatest joy. In this chapter, in their own words, teachers tell why they love teaching and what they do to help their students deal with stress.

The Joys of Teaching

Helping students learn

Teachers experience joy when they see that they have helped foster a love of learning in their students. Jason bursts into the room with a library book by an author we have studied and insists that I read it to the class. Lindsay, while looking for reference books for an animal inquiry, indignantly states, "Can you believe it? This book doesn't even have an index!" Chris scoots up to the front of the group as I start reading and whispers loudly, "Quiet, she's reading!"

> I feel joy when after every read-aloud a child says, "I thought that [the last book] was the best book I ever read, but this one is really the best one." I know what they mean. It is the joy of sharing the pleasure of good literature. I feel joy when we have shared a joke or a tear.
>
> *Fifth-grade teacher, South Dakota*

We have all had *Aha* moments when we're working hard to explain a concept and all at once we hit upon the correct match between our teaching and a child's learning. Then the student says, "Oh, I get it," and rushes off to continue working because she doesn't need us any more.

> I feel great joy when I help a child meet an academic or social challenge that seemed insurmountable a moment before. I feel joy when I see the AHA light in a child's eyes. I feel joy when they say, "Oh, this is so EASY." I know then that I have done my job well.
>
> *Fifth-grade teacher, South Dakota*

But is it so easy? One teacher suggested that often the greatest joy of learning something new is accompanied by great anxiety, and questioned whether we can have one without the other. I found that in some teaching-learning situations there was a healthy anxiety or tension, when the students and I were stretching ourselves because we wanted the same result. We were involved in what Renate Caine and Geoffrey Caine, researchers on the brain and optimal learning situations, call "high rigor, low stress" situations (1991). At these times, our risk and vulnerability was protected by the trust and caring we had developed together.

I remember how Curtis persevered in practicing *Teammates* by Peter Golenbock so he could read it in front of the class. The book was clearly beyond his instructional level, but Curtis was motivated to work through it, and he did. I had to draw upon all my knowledge of teaching reading, all my strategies for encouraging and supporting students, as well as my own patience, as I worked with him. Then one day, he said he was ready, and he read the first page to his classmates. At the end of the page, he let out a long sigh, gave a big smile and said that that was all he was going to read. The tension was gone, replaced by deep satisfaction. Curtis returned to reading more suitable books on his reading level, as well as working to read *Teammates*, and he never again asked me to help him with it.

The apparent ease of learning comes after repeated exposure to a concept and after varied opportunities to explore a text. Children often surprise us with the depth of their understanding, when unintended learning happens and they show us something they have learned that was not part of our lesson plan. When we're open to new possibilities, our students will lead us to new areas of learning and different ways of teaching.

> I find joy when we revisit an idea or concept in order to develop it further and the children go beyond my expectations. For example, when we work on varying sentence structures during guided writing and then during independent writing time, a student who has been writing only one word starts writing sentences. Or when a child who is still an emergent reader at the middle of first grade picks out a sophisticated relationship between characters that his fluent reading friends didn't see.
>
> *First-grade teacher, California*

Sometimes, such as this high school math teacher in Minnesota, we use humor to teach.

> I feel the best as a teacher when a student appreciates and recognizes that I am truly trying to help her. I feel great when a student understands for the first time or when the class is not understanding

the material initially and then I explain the math in a goofy way that really makes sense to them.

High school math teacher, Minnesota

Learning in a caring community

The joy that teachers feel as their students learn is embedded in the caring classroom community that they create together. Teachers know that the most long-lasting learning takes place when their students feel confident, when they are able to take risks, and when they work in a positive atmosphere. This is not a frill or an add-on, but a deeply held belief that comes from their center. It is reinforced by their home, school, and community experiences. It continues to strengthen through the daily emotional, social, intellectual, physical, and spiritual growth of their students.

I feel terrific when there is a sense of community in the classroom. This is when students accept each other and the diversity becomes a positive rather than a lingering negative. When the bully, clown, or wallflower finds his/her voice beyond that stereotype.

Kindergarten teacher, Pennsylvania

I know that children are learning when they are really working together on a project and using the caring language we talk about so often, helping each other out, sharing, etc.

First-grade teacher, Oregon

When the community is working in harmony, we can easily understand Frank Smith's comment that learning is easy (1995). We see our students as self-motivated, self-monitoring learners, knowing what they need to do next and knowing what they need from us as teachers.

I find the most joyful part of teaching is the time when my students are on target and involved in the project at hand. Their enthusiasm glows outward and I know they are thriving on that thrill of total involvement as they are, maybe unknowingly, learning. At these times I can clearly see my learning disabled and developmentally handicapped students developing skills finally over a long period of work and time.

Grades 1–3 Resource Room teacher, Ohio

Learning from our students

At times we can step back for a moment and see what our students are learning. These kid-watching opportunities become the authentic assessment we use to plan further lessons and learning experiences. Our students become our best teachers.

> Joy for me comes with watching children learn, try out roles or situations for themselves, and take risks—when a shy child learns the right words to use to stand up for him or herself, when a child yells out an answer which surprises me in its insight.
>
> *First-grade teacher, Arizona*

> I feel the most joy when I notice the change in my students' levels of knowing. When I can tell that they are "getting it." When I feel that we have flow in the classroom because the kids are getting excited about pursuing their own knowledge. When I learn something or see something in a new way, try something different with my children, and it works! Or when the children demonstrate their knowing to me and I am surprised at how much they have learned.
>
> There is also joy in my teaching when my students let me into their world of perceptions. One day when I was searching for the yardstick to introduce it as another measuring tool, a student asked, "What's a yardstick?" Another student replied, "You know, it's one of those special sticks you put in your backyard."
>
> *Kindergarten teacher, Montana*

Feeling centered

These stories of the joy of teaching speak to times when teachers feel centered. At the moment they feel a joy, peace, and balance.

> Being centered is knowing what I believe and how to implement it. It is a calmness inside of me. I have a clear vision of what I want the students to learn and do. Many times things don't work as planned and that's okay as long as I keep the vision clearly in mind. My voice gets softer, allowing other voices to grow louder.
>
> *Elementary language arts consultant, Minnesota*

> Those magic moments when the class and I were together, when we formed a close and precious community spurred either by an

outside event or the power of our academic pursuits. Times I could be myself in the classroom and learn and love along with my students contributed enormously to my own growth and joy.

High school English teacher, California

Helping Students Deal with Stress

In the learning experiences described above, in which teachers felt the joy of teaching, neither they nor the students were unduly stressed. Teachers work hard to create those situations, knowing that children develop as successful learners and healthy citizens when active learning is accompanied by low stress. Maintaining caring learning communities that provide opportunities for everyone to feel centered and balanced requires that we help our students deal with stress.

Stress impedes our students' intellectual, social, emotional, physical, and spiritual growth. Children can be stressed about their schoolwork, about relationships with friends and adults, and about their home situations. If a child is hungry, he can't concentrate. If a child is without friends, she is lonely. If a child is distracted, he can't learn well. When a child worries about her home life, she searches for answers from people at school. We know that we have to address these issues in order to create classroom environments with high rigor, low stress.

I asked teachers, "How do you help your students deal with stress?" As shown in the following list, some teachers described specific approaches that focus on classroom environment and daily schedule, teaching strategies, talking and listening, or relaxation techniques. Others responded with a general description of their classroom community, in which all aspects were integrated.

Helping Students Deal with Stress

- Since I teach kindergarten, one thing I can do is pick them up or hold them on my lap.
- Try to make my classroom a haven of peace.
- Teach the kids to use polite manners.
- Help my students learn how to problem solve interpersonal difficulties.

Helping Students Deal with Stress (*continued*)

- Teach them how to nurture each other.
- Use a quiet voice when I sense the stress level rising.
- Take one-minute "rests" to quiet ourselves when necessary.
- Plan lessons that are fun and challenging, but open-ended, so kids can take them as far as they are able.
- Do a lot of partner and group work, so the students can help each other accomplish goals.
- Balance challenging material with activities such as singing, playing outside, and artwork.
- Get to know each child personally; I believe that our relationship eases their stress.
- Have frequent contact with the parents of my students, in order to keep all parties informed and involved in the child's educational process. Sometimes a word to or from a parent is all it takes to relieve a child's stress.
- Play classical music.
- Practice relaxation techniques after recess.

Classroom environment and daily schedule

Teachers can create an emotionally supportive atmosphere that children can count on from day to day. Specific ground rules and procedures form the foundation for this learning environment.

> I try first to set up a nonstressful type atmosphere in the classroom. I try to give my students choice about their own learning and not to anger them with "having" to do what I think is important. At the same time I still let them know what work I feel is important for them to do. We talk a lot about feelings, procedures, and expected behaviors. I try not to let the children's stress become my own, but sometimes I am not too successful. I know that if I can keep myself happy and centered the children seem to catch that feeling.
>
> *Fifth-grade teacher, South Dakota*

When I was teaching kindergarten and first grade, I organized the physical arrangement of my classroom in order to foster rigorous learning and low stress. I had science, social studies, and math areas, where my students could explore, experiment, read, and write about the physical world. I provided a variety of writing and art materials that were available for the children to record what they were learning. I arranged the room so children could relax in quiet places throughout the room.

I set up a flexible daily schedule that children could depend on day to day. I balanced active times (such as project work) with quiet times (independent reading), and whole class learning (shared reading) with group work (creating a social studies mural) or independent pursuits (painting a picture). I scheduled passive experiences (listening to a story), followed by more intensive active learning times (writing a story).

> I think the way that I help my students deal with stress is by giving them encouragement and the space and time to explore learning. I think I give my students the message that they are capable and intelligent people. I allow children to go at their own pace. I think this helps them manage stress, at least I hope it does.
>
> *First-grade teacher, Ecuador*

Teachers are aware that their students' busy and stressful lives often make it difficult for them to get their school assignments done. A middle school social studies teacher tells how she helps her students organize their work when they get behind or feel overwhelmed.

> My students are always welcome to come to me and tell me that many things are going on and that they feel too overburdened. We then sit down and compose a schedule that maps out how and when they will get the work done. They may have extensions on assignments if it is necessary. Also, I remind myself that these students have lives outside of school. They have conflicts at home and other stresses that come with them to school.
>
> *Middle school social studies teacher, New York*

> I try to keep the classroom well-organized and lessons planned out to give plenty of time in class for my students to complete work for the next day.
>
> *Middle school science teacher, Minnesota*

Teaching strategies

One of our jobs is to create those joyful *Aha!* times: to help a child work through a science experiment; to find one more way to explain a math concept; to discover just the right book to inspire a child to read; to orchestrate a readers' theatre so that Shakespeare comes to the center stage of an English class; or to set up a mock trial to bring Aristotle alive for social studies students. This is hard work, and assumes balancing different tasks, but it is the joy of teaching.

One obvious source of stress is when students don't know what they are trying to learn. Thoughtful teachers make certain that their students understand the learning context at the beginning, as well as throughout the lesson.

> I help my students deal with stress by helping them understand and figure out what they really want to know and the questions they were really asking.
>
> *High school English teacher, California*

Teachers get to know the specific stress of individual students, and make accommodations to help them.

> I try to be aware of their individual stresses and create an environment that is low risk. I had one student, Alex, who got very stressed whenever a new concept was introduced. So I knew that I had to spend some individual time with him at the beginning of the task and encourage him along the way.
>
> *Kindergarten teacher, Michigan*

Teachers also are sensitive to the learning styles, personalities, and interests of their students. The following story demonstrates what happens when students truly value their own work.

> Anthony spent much of his time inventing ways not to do his work. He often forgot homework, had trouble completing projects, and reported that he found schoolwork boring. I did my best to make school meaningful for him, but my efforts rarely made a difference. In the spring, we were studying ancient China and I asked the students to choose any aspect of the society to serve as

the basis of a project. Anthony chose fireworks—and I've never seen him more excited. He ran into class every day to show me pictures, articles, and models of fireworks that he had found. He showed his classmates what he'd discovered and constantly asked them for ideas about where he could find more. He would ask, "When are we going to have social studies?" Anthony's work in other subject areas improved too. He was on a mission—to become our class expert on fireworks. Anthony's final presentation was clear and thorough, and included diagrams, research, and even a little bit of information on China. Later in the spring, during parent conferences, Anthony asked if he could give his presentation again to his parents. Both he and his parents were proud of his accomplishments. Although Anthony ended up forgetting, for the most part, that he was supposed to focus on China, he learned a great deal about research, and about his own intellectual abilities.

Sixth-grade teacher, Illinois

Teachers provide time outside of class to help their students. They report that everyone benefits from this individual contact, which emphasizes the importance of mutual trust and respect in teaching.

I try to provide opportunities for students to be successful, such as help sessions when they can drop in for extra help on things that they don't understand. I try to make them feel at ease even when they may not like the subject matter. I tell them that they must plod through it, but that I will try to make it as interesting as possible. I let them know when something is going to be hard and when it's going to be easy so that they learn to trust me as a teacher. I really put some effort into listening when I know that the subject is really hard. I get on a more personal level with my students so we can build mutual respect. I want them to realize that I am there to help them learn something that I am knowledgeable about.

Middle school math teacher, Minnesota

Listening and talking

Teachers reported that one of the ways they help their students deal with stress is by listening to and talking with them. From experience, they know that personal problems and school-related situations can undermine the classroom community and interfere with learning if they don't help their students learn to address them.

I have found that talking to a student, face to face, eyeball to eyeball, is the best way to help them deal with stress. I also use my personal life to show them that everybody makes mistakes, gets sick, gets grumpy, is happy, etc. They love knowing that I am real, just like them, and that I understand what they tell me and show me. They love knowing what my ten-year-old son does, too.

Kindergarten teacher, Pennsylvania

I read a story that relates to their stress and talk with them about it, talk about stories we have read or experiences we have had together that relate to their stress and how to resolve it.

First-grade teacher, Michigan

There seem to be many opportunities for open communication in elementary classrooms because usually the teacher is with the same group of children all day. But teachers of middle and high school students, with whom they meet for a shorter amount of time each day, can also create trust.

I have a strong bond with my students. I feel we have an open communication with each other. Communication is important in our classroom. My favorite saying to the kids when stressed about homework or other academic areas is "It's no big deal. We will manage." I show my students the same compassion I would like my daughter to receive from her teacher. It keeps it in perspective for me.

Middle school teacher, California

Every day I work with individual students to praise and challenge them. Now I have a relationship with them and they know I do in fact care deeply and individually about them, I can challenge them to work harder.

High school teacher, Washington, DC

Many teachers use a class meeting forum to help solve stressful issues that arise within the classroom community. The biweekly class meetings in my first grade had two focuses: problems that came up in the normal course of the day (such as how to share the classroom ball at recess), and general procedures, rules, and skills that would help us be a more productive learning and caring community (such as ways to be a good listener).

> We have weekly class meetings where students can voice concerns and anxieties. I also think that self-reflective writing and one-to-one meetings all help students reduce stress. Most important, though, is making myself accessible and listening—listening well to them. Early on, I help students understand that they can talk to me without fear of me judging them.
>
> *Middle school teacher, Virginia*

Although they can't always separate personal problems from school-related issues, teachers are careful to keep their roles clear. They are not psychologists or therapists and must be aware of situations when they need to encourage a student to seek professional help. Their job is to teach, and in order for learning to take place they must keep the classroom a safe, supportive place to learn.

> I empathize with their home life situations instead of sympathize with them. My students know that I'm a good listener. Sometimes when they bring in stresses from home, I simply lend my ear, and tell them how much I understand their feelings toward their situation. I have learned (after many sleepless nights) that I cannot "change" their home lives.
>
> *First-grade teacher, California*

> I let them know that we all have stresses; that I understand; that they can write to me in their journal about it; that I will listen. LISTEN! I don't find that sharing any specific personal stress is at all helpful, because that is talk, not listening, and does not really meet their needs. Listening helps, and just caring. I remember how teachers helped me when I was young, and it was by letting me know I was valued—by listening to me, believing me, and affirming my competence. Some teachers were patronizing, and that was worse than being ignored or snubbed.
>
> *Elementary curriculum specialist, California*

Sometimes teachers help their students deal with stressful school situations that arise outside their classroom community. It takes skill and sensitivity on their part to help students negotiate with the schoolwide policies and personnel, as demonstrated in the following story.

> My students often expressed their frustrations with school policies (e.g., no talking during lunch, no bringing books into the classroom unless they are specifically assigned by the teacher) and other situations they encountered which they felt were unfair. I would ask them to consider their options in the situation and decide what made the most sense. Role-playing often worked well. Students could role-play asking their teacher why they could not bring "outside" books into class—and consider the possible consequences. Then they could make their own decisions and feel, more or less, comfortable with whatever happened.
>
> *Sixth-grade teacher, Illinois*

Relaxing strategies and TLC

Teachers know that in order for learning to happen they need to incorporate relaxing moments into the fabric of their classroom community. Many of these moments are short and integrate easily into the flow of the day. I used to have my students take a few deep breaths as they settled down to independent reading after recess. A teacher I know leads her class with ten minutes of relaxation techniques when they come in from lunch. Other instances of TLC are as quick and easy as giving a tap on the head or a smile.

> To help students deal with stress we try breathing exercises or we rub the sides of our temples—to wake up our brains. I have also played quiet soothing classical music during tests to relieve stress and create a more peaceful, pleasant atmosphere. I recommend playing the CD "Mozart Makes You Smarter."
>
> *First-grade teacher, Ohio*

It is well-known that physical exercise is an excellent stress reducer for children, as well as adults. Young children need to get outside and run around with their peers. In elementary classrooms, where children

21

are with the same teacher and group of children all day, it is especially important that they get exercise in a bigger space, preferably outside. When teachers join their students outside, they have added opportunities to observe them in social situations and talk with them in a more relaxed manner.

> I take the children outside as often as I can throughout the year. I get the opportunity to interact more with some of the children who need my attention in a less threatening atmosphere for them. Outside, there seems to be less to fight over—no favorite pen or pencil, no particular crayon, no harried teacher. We have no playground equipment so the children make up their own games, play at being joggers on the track and climb a wonderful old tree that bends low to the ground seemingly just for them.
>
> *First-grade teacher, Michigan*

Caring community

The ways that teachers help their students deal with stress are not isolated strategies. Rather, they are the result of the teachers' visions of caring classroom communities that they create in partnership with the students. Nel Noddings, in her extensive work on caring in schools, claims, "When we discuss teaching and teacher-learner relationships in depth, we will see that teachers not only have to create caring relations in which they are the carers, but that they also have a responsibility to help their students develop the capacity to care" (1992, 18).

> I think it is most important to let them know that you are there for them in any capacity they need you. Some kids need to be close, some need their space. Some need to spend more time on the playground, or the whole time on a pillow in the library area. I think that each child will show you what it is they need and the most important thing we can do is let it happen.
>
> *Preschool teacher, Ohio*

> My classroom has many different areas where children can go to spend quiet time alone. Offering time alone with the children to read a book, snuggle up to just let them know they are important, and hugs every day seem to have become crucial in our classroom.

We also have many class meetings that address ways to deal with specific situations as they arise. Keeping a close community seems to be the best way to help children through stressful situations. Pull together is my motto.

First-grade teacher, Arizona

I play calming music while they are writing, and at other times in the day. We do a lot of talking about trying our best and that our best is all we can give; but as I think now, I guess I really don't make a purposeful effort to "teach kids" to deal with the many stresses they have in their little lives. I know many do have quite a few stresses.

First -grade teacher, Oregon

Students bring great joy, but they also bring great stress and challenge. In the next chapters, teachers describe some of these stresses and discuss ways that they meet these challenges when they are "feeling frantic inside," and offer suggestions of ways to remedy difficult situations.

3

School Community

THE SCHOOL community plays an important role in successful teaching and learning. Stress is reduced and learning is elevated when school atmosphere fosters respect and trust, when building facilities are clean and functional, and when materials are readily available. The teachers I spoke with listed many stressful teaching situations and suggested many ways in which their school environments could be improved.

School Community

School atmosphere

A positive school atmosphere helps teachers stay centered. When trust and respect break down among school staff, teachers' energy is siphoned off from the positive work of teaching and is spent dealing with negative relationships that include gossip, criticism, faultfinding, judgments, competition, and one-upmanship. In this environment, teachers find themselves isolated and in an atmosphere of competition, and they must expend an excessive amount of time and energy trying to keep centered and balanced.

> There is too much gossip at my school. People trade trust just to get a little "scoop." Despising it, after three years I am now hearing some of it just because people know I can be trusted not to share. Gossip can undermine a staff. My principal promotes it!
>
> *First-grade teacher, California*

It is difficult to create a caring classroom and optimum learning environment when we teach in an "angry, punishment-driven school environment." Closing our door is not an adequate solution.

> I try to close my classroom door to the angry, punishment-driven environment in my school, but it seems impossible. The children experience it in the lunchroom, during bathroom time, and at home. It permeates their relationship to the world. I'm constantly struggling with myself to overcome the frustrations of large class size and the students' poor social skills that lead me to go with the models around me, and the ones the children are most familiar with.
>
> *First-grade teacher, Michigan*

Schools ought to be places where teachers and administrators talk together about teaching and learning. We grow when we are able to express our opinions in a listening environment and reflect on our practice. The following teacher would have benefited from a collegial environment in which all opinions were respected and heard. The school in which she was teaching would have benefited from a principal who could create a learning environment that encouraged honest discussion and who held staff accountable for their comments.

> My colleagues and I often differed regarding our teaching philosophies and approaches to instruction. I worked hard to achieve a classroom environment based on mutual trust in which students had real input in all areas—from deciding what to study and how to go about learning it to creating our classroom rules (or Class Constitution). My colleagues tended to believe the "official" curriculum and "official" rules should dominate. I often felt they regarded me with suspicion or, at best, the belief that, as a new teacher, I was naive in my belief that children should have so much responsibility. At faculty meetings, I sometimes took on my colleagues, sometimes stayed quiet—depending on the issue and my energy level. I remember one meeting when a colleague who taught middle school history stated, "Look, I think the textbook is boring too. But sometimes learning has to hurt." I learned a great deal from these interactions—because they challenged

me to articulate what I believed as an educator, and what I was willing to fight for.

Sixth-grade teacher, Illinois

It is a special challenge to create a school community in large schools, where often there is no common teachers' room, entrance door, or lunchtime. From day to day teachers only see colleagues who teach in their same hall. Most teachers have twenty-five minutes for lunch, which is often spent getting their students to and from lunch, preparing for their next class, using the copy machine, or calling a parent. It takes tremendous effort and commitment for a teacher to take the time to sit down and eat with colleagues.

Teachers' Suggestions for Principals to Enhance School Atmosphere

- In assemblies with primary students, please remember their developmental stage and don't lecture to them for long periods of time, expecting that I will keep them under control. If there is a problem, perhaps ask the classes to come up with presentations about how to solve the problem.
- Train lunch aides so they don't scream and so they learn means of keeping order with active children other than physical punishment.
- Don't put so much emphasis on punishment. Instead, develop programs that bring the students, staff, and parents together as a community to celebrate accomplishments.
- Find ways to bring programs to the school that give students who may excel at nonacademic things the opportunity to do so.
- Show your presence in every classroom every day in a positive manner.
- Encourage risk-taking by teachers and students. Help teams of teachers who want to try something different develop a means and schedule for assessing, revising, and reassessing their attempts.
- Don't interrupt with intercom accouncements.

Suggestions to Enhance School Atmosphere *(continued)*

- Take a stand against policies that are not good for kids and teachers.
- Be a substitute in our classrooms.
- Learn more about teaching, so you can be a teacher leader, not a distant politician.
- Come into our classrooms. Get to know our kids, and share in our joys and struggles.

I teach in a large school—twelve-hundred students and sixty-five teachers pre-K through 8. I try eating lunch in different places in the school since different groups seem to gather for lunch in various classrooms. After about four years here I still have not found where the third- and fourth-grade teachers gather, if they do. It is difficult to impossible to develop collegial relationships. Last year for about three months I organized a small study group of teachers. Usually only two people attended each biweekly meeting—another teacher and I—though very seldom the same teacher. We continued this the following summer and had four consistent participants though most did not read the material we had chosen together.

First-grade teacher, Michigan

Facilities

Inadequate facilities add to teachers' stresses and undermine their ability to teach. The disparity among facilities in different school systems, which Jonathan Kozol describes in *Savage Inequalities*, is widespread. One high school teacher in an inner city reported that her classroom gets swept once every couple of weeks. Time and time again teachers mentioned that they teach in building facilities that are in disrepair. When asked how she deals with this, one teacher wrote, "Keeping a sense of humor helps." It is a sad commentary that she could offer no other suggestion.

The library ought to be the hub of the school, and yet some schools have no library facilities, or libraries that are inadequate or inaccessible. Most teachers spend a great deal of their own money to build classroom libraries and make books available to their students. The following description is representative of what many teachers do.

> Our school librarian has decided that the library is for the middle school students and won't spend the money for materials for the primary students. I have had to build my own first- and second-grade classroom library. I get books from resale shops as well as buy new books. I send out permission slips at the beginning of the year, which the parents and children must sign accepting responsibility for the books that go home and agreeing to pay to replace lost or irreparable ones they have signed out. I also bring my own computer into class for the children to use.
>
> *Primary teacher, Michigan*

> Last year in second grade I arranged for a field trip every three weeks to take us to the public library. I chose the main branch as it is in the cultural center so for the same amount of money we walked to the art museum, children's museum, and historical museum. For some extra money for the entrance fee we visited the Museum of African American History.
>
> *First-grade teacher, Michigan*

Nonteaching tasks

Teachers are expected to spend time planning for their students, writing report cards, meeting with parents, and attending staff and curriculum meetings. Since very little of this can be done during the day while the children are in school, these nonteaching tasks have to be done before and after school, as well as on weekends and vacations. Excessive and unreasonable nonteaching demands, however, add stress and detract from teaching.

> I am stressed by all the documentations, stuff from the main office, administration office, curriculum, etc. All this takes time and there is precious little time to do it all at school.
>
> *First-grade teacher, Ohio*

> I'm stressed by the number of interruptions I experience during my contact time with the kids. I am interrupted for phone calls and messages, to go to assemblies, do vision and hearing screening,

provide fluoride tablets to the kids, etc. These things can disrupt the flow of a lesson, distract the kids, and unnecessarily limit the contact time I have with the kids.

Kindergarten teacher, Oregon

I find report card time stressful because I need to update factual assessments, as well as keep up with classwork. We do, fortunately, get one day off to write the reports. I deal with these by trying to keep myself really organized, and because I only teach half time, I try to make a point of not spending any more time at school without the students than I do with them—not more than five hours a day.

First-grade teacher, Canada

Teachers are willing to meet with other teachers to share ideas and reflect on their practice, but they find it stressful to waste time at staff meetings that don't serve their needs.

Another stress is the lack of time to meet with other teachers of my own grade level. Most staff meeting agenda items do not apply to kindergarten teachers or their classes, and yet I am required to sit through these meetings with the other kindergarten teachers, not productively planning curriculum or brainstorming solutions to problems, but just passing the time. On the days not designated as meetings for the entire staff, we are required to meet as teams, k–3 or 4–5. Although sometimes it is helpful to have the team meetings, usually this is also not time best spent. Instead, we need weekly time to meet with other teachers of our own grade levels.

Kindergarten teacher, Oregon

I seem to be spending a tremendous amount of time after and before school in meetings, collaborating with colleagues, designing curriculum, reinventing the wheel, rewriting report cards, discussing how to change our schedules, talking about assessment, parental involvement, whole school projects, our environmental program, etc. Sometimes I feel so overloaded with the "other things" that involve being a teacher that I feel I am spending less time on planning for just my 20 kindergartners.

Kindergarten teacher, Indiana

I want to focus all I've learned in my past six years of teaching on my own classroom. I have grown weary of writing great lessons a substitute gets to carry out because I am at meetings.

Second-grade teacher, California

Frequently, new programs and content areas are added to an already full curriculum, and teachers have little, if any, say in the decision making process. Nothing is taken away and teachers are expected to fit it in the best they can, and yet are held accountable for it. Planning time or inservice for new programs is not offered, and often appropriate materials are not provided. These new curriculum programs are often introduced by state legislatures, school committee members, or administrators who are unaware of the everyday demands of the classroom. When teachers are not included in the decision making, it is more difficult to integrate a new program with the rest of the curriculum.

I think some stress comes from the amount of time we as teachers are required to spend on specific content or areas in a curriculum that does not lend itself well to be integrated. We are constantly given more to teach, lip service to assistance, and more and more paperwork and assessments to be completed. Not only are we expected to teach more in an already tight schedule, but we are expected to take on the additional preparation and evaluation time outside the classroom. When we are not asked to teach more, we are asked to give up our precious time for special programs to come in. Many times orders masquerade as requests or choices. Lack of time for reading and math instruction certainly creates adverse conditions!

First-grade teacher, California

There is too much work to do and too little time in which to do it. By this I refer both to the teacher workload outside of contact time with the kids, as well as the little amount of contact time available relative to the huge job of teaching the kids what they need to know. I'm always having to make choices, to try to balance the curriculum, knowing that on any given day, I'm leaving out important parts of the curriculum.

Kindergarten teacher, Oregon

Teachers' Suggestions for School Administrators

- Manage limited funds carefully so that they are spent where teachers need them, not where "things will look good."
- Announce assemblies in advance—perhaps at the beginning of each week, at least a week in advance.
- Don't just tell or remind, but *invite* parents to school functions and parent-teacher conferences. Find a way to acknowledge their interest and the time they took to come.
- Keep unimportant stuff out of staff meetings, so we can maximize our time to prepare our instruction.
- Place everyone who is at the same grade level in adjacent rooms in order to facilitate team planning.
- Deflect as much of the politics as possible, not raising our alarm until a situation absolutely requires it.
- Think carefully about what is inferred to be politically correct, and choose wisely when asking us to jump on a bandwagon.
- Work with me and other teachers to change the reporting procedure in primary grades to eliminate letter grades and institute a system that will better demonstrate a child's progress and development.
- When you pay me to go to a workshop on inquiry-based learning and constructivism, please don't tell me I can't apply what I've learned until after my students have completed all the required math worksheets that are antithetical to what I learned at the workshop.
- Consider teachers as part of your team. Meet with them, look at the budget together, and find ways to lower class sizes together.
- At staff meetings, don't talk *at* us. Much of what you say can be written in a memo. Allow time for discussion and allow teachers to add agenda items as necessary.
- Don't tell me to fill out a purchase order for things I would like and then tell me we don't have the money for any of them.

Suggestions for School Administrators (*continued*)

- If you require me to give photocopied homework sheets three times each week, allow me access to the copy machine and paper or make sure someone gets the copies made for me each week so I don't have to go to a copy store on my own time and pay for it with my own money.

- Have the school secretaries keep class lists on their computers. When a student transfers, they should make the change on their own lists instead of asking me over the intercom during class to send an updated list to the office.

Coping Strategies

Teachers are extremely resourceful in working out ways to cope with stressful aspects that are created outside their classroom.

I find that my stress level decreases greatly when I take a few minutes to "talk" through my lesson plans. Either in the car on the way or when I arrive I silently go through the schedule for the day and make a mental note of activities that are planned and changes that might occur. This quick activity is calming for me. It reminds me of the routine and helps me to more effectively manage my time. It also helps me to prepare for the inevitable interruptions in our day. I find that when I take the time to do this I am calmer and much more effective as an educator.

Kindergarten teacher, Alabama

Can you believe that my administration doesn't feel recess is necessary or appropriate for kindergarten since each session is only there for 2 hours and 35 minutes? So, I call it gross outdoor motor exploration and go out as often as I can. I also have my own piano in the classroom and use music on a daily basis.

Kindergarten teacher, New Hampshire

My specific stresses in teaching are: lack of parental support; meeting all of students' individual needs at the same time; working with our state's graduation standards performance packages; planning, implementing, and getting students enthused to do work; and trying to answer parent questions as best I can. How do I deal with the above issues? I work to keep parents informed and involved in student responsibility and discipline. I do what I can and if I don't get the support I need, I seek the administration's help or I think of avenues for the student to have choices that we both can live with. I also try to keep a fairly structured classroom with lesson plans posted at least a week at a time on a board so students can work through things together, rather than always asking me for the answers.

High school teacher, Minnesota

What helps the most is to keep a daily journal of what went on in class, how I felt about it, dealt with it, what I would like to do differently next time. I keep reminding myself that I am human, in the process of learning, in a difficult situation, and will usually have another chance. Whatever happened today will probably happen again sometime so I can think about it and do it better next time. I also find it is helpful, when I feel we have really gotten away from being a caring community, to put aside the daily routine and do something different. Sometimes it is a class meeting to discuss what we are all feeling and how to make it better. Sometimes I call it a workshop day (usually a half day) and the kids can choose independently what they want to do. We have a brief meeting about how this will look so that everyone is happy and safe. When I do this I look around as I work with individuals and think, "Why can't we do this every day?" I guess I still do worry about what the administration wants me to do and am not yet confident that I can organize minilessons and assessments within this structure to satisfy their expectations.

First-grade teacher, Michigan

Another important factor is laughter. Most of the third-grade teachers share a lunch, far from the politics of the faculty lunchroom. We joke, laugh, and relax together during that half hour. We rarely eat cafeteria food, and we celebrate birthdays with great lunches. This camaraderie renews us during the workday.

Third-grade teacher, New York

I also have let a lot of things "go." I ask myself how much it matters in the big scheme of things. I am not nearly as controlling as I used to be. I have learned to delegate, to kids and to parent helpers. If it doesn't turn out the same way I would have done it, it is okay. I am also starting yoga; I just got a video to help me.

Kindergarten teacher, Ohio

Suggestions

Teachers have many suggestions about ways that school community can be improved so that they can devote their time to teaching their students. In response to my question, "What can be done to reduce the nonteaching tasks and increasing curriculum demands that take away from your planning and teaching time?" the following teacher had several suggestions.

First of all, they could get current in technology so that repetitive clerical tasks could be automated and streamlined as much as possible. Second, they could offer to take the class for a half day so you could focus on portfolios or curriculum planning. Third, they could get input from teachers when they schedule specialists to enable collaborative planning among grade levels. Fourth, they could work toward team teaching, job sharing, hiring more aides and volunteers to do recess and lunch duty.

Kindergarten teacher, Nebraska

A teacher union in one district has proposed negotiating some limits on required unpaid duties that take up excessive teacher time away from teaching.

Currently we are engaged with the district negotiators in writing the district's first-ever job description for teachers. Our idea is that once we define the core responsibilities, then everything else is by definition extra duties and can either be paid, eliminated, or assigned to nonteaching staff or to volunteers. Some core responsibilities are:

1. engaging and supporting all students in learning
2. creating and maintaining effective environments for student learning

3. understanding and organizing subject matter for student learning
4. planning instruction and designing learning experiences for all students
5. assessing student learning
6. developing as a professional educator

Second-grade teacher, California

Most teachers don't require major changes—they simply ask for respect and collegiality from administrators.

Teachers' Suggestions for Principals for Relating to Individual Teachers

- If you call me in for a conference, please let me know the topic so I can come prepared.
- If you have concerns about my conduct or my teaching, please express them to me in private rather than announce them during a conference with a parent or with other teachers.
* If you hear something you don't like about me, come and see for yourself.
- If I'm doing a good job, tell me. Fire poor teachers who make life so difficult for kids and fellow teachers.
- Do not require me to have a grade for each student for each week for each subject. If you are concerned about my assessment and evaluation, you may look at my copious anecdotal records and other types of assessment and evaluation that give me a picture of where each child is and what I need to do next for each child.
- Allow me to write lesson plans that help me to teach rather than require me to write plans that follow someone else's prescription. If there is a problem about my teaching, it will not show up in my lesson plans.

4

Students and Parents

> One of the biggest stressors for me was dealing with unreasonable parents and intimidating children. I think they can smell fear and their natural response is to attack.
>
> *Elementary staff developer, California*

WE HAVE seen that the joy of teaching comes from helping students learn and that teachers work hard to develop a stress-free classroom environment to foster learning. This is not an easy task, and teachers often must confront incredible odds to maintain a positive learning atmosphere in their classrooms. Sometimes they are successful, but many times teachers have to settle for less than they would like. Teachers want to make a difference in their students' lives and find it hard to accept that there are difficult circumstances with challenging students and parents over which they have little or no control.

> The stresses can be many, but usually it always gets back to the children! I worry, "Are they making enough progress for their ability?" "Am I pushing too hard, not enough?" "What will I do with the one or two children with whose parents I can't seem to make any real connecting contact? They don't send back reading envelopes, never come to school functions, etc." To deal with these stresses, I usually need to put things in perspective and abandon the "save the world" mentality. I have to realize that while I can't give up on any particular child, I do have to set my limits, too.

There are only so many times I can prompt, encourage, and re-mind the child, not to mention calling home and sending notes. Talking with my teammates, who are wonderful, really helps me download. We listen to each other. And it saves my husband's ear!

First-grade teacher, Oregon

Students

Experiences in the elementary grades

Teachers report that they are experiencing an increase of discipline problems that disrupt their teaching and add stress to everyone in the class. As they continue to care for these children, they question whether they can teach effectively amid the many interruptions of cer-tain children.

Another set of problems arises from students with behavioral is-sues. Many times the lesson is interrupted because of the outbursts of the few very problematic children in my class. At issue is not whether I can teach them or love them. Of course I can and do both of these things, but the question is whether maintaining the status quo is in the best interest of the children, the "problem" ones included. Last year, I was kicked hard in the shins almost every day by a severely disturbed child (who also had a habit of laying on girls and thrusting himself, telling them that they were sexy—and this in kindergarten!). It takes so long to document the problem, try the classroom interventions, and to convince the powers that be that these children would be best served in an alternate setting, such as a program for severely emotionally disturbed children, or a developmental kindergarten. Then, once the work has been done (and perhaps a year has passed), you learn that even though he qualifies, there is no opening in the program.

Kindergarten teacher, Oregon

Unfortunately, some children arrive at school with problems that make it difficult for them to learn—their home lives do not support their literacy learning in school, they lack proper nutrition, their parents are too consumed with their own survival to give them the nurturing and school support they need, or they have learning disabilities and need special help that schools are unable to provide. Often the classroom teacher is left alone to juggle both attending to the personal needs of her students as well as covering the class itself.

> My experience has been working mostly with disadvantaged children inside Title I schools, and I find that too many children come to school incredibly ill-prepared. It becomes a yearlong challenging journey of getting them from point "A to Z."
>
> *Kindergarten teacher, Wyoming*

> Some desperately need psychological counseling due to abusive home situations. Some need lots more time with an adult than I can provide.
>
> *First-grade teacher, Michigan*

An increasing number of children with extreme special needs are being mainstreamed into regular classrooms. These include children with Down's syndrome, autism, severe emotional problems, and physical disabilities. When an inclusion child is mainstreamed appropriately through the collaborative effort of the schoolwide team and the child's primary caregivers, everyone gains from the experience. First of all, the team needs to decide if the child will benefit from being mainstreamed, or if he or she will be more successful in a more restrictive environment. Secondly, the team should make certain that the learning environment will not be compromised for the rest of the children in the class. Finally, the team must ensure that the teacher receives the needed support. This generally would include a full-time qualified classroom assistant who is charged with helping the child so that the teacher can attend to teaching the class.

Unfortunately, when this assistance isn't in place, the teacher is left with the responsibility for the regular class members, as well as for the inclusion child who needs one-on-one help. Without thoughtful planning and commitment from the schoolwide team, the teacher is left with a responsibility far beyond the capabilities of one person. Inclusion is a very complex issue, as described in the following comments about the difficulties and the joys of inclusion students.

Ten years ago I began teaching inclusion, before the word *inclusion* was coined. It was the biggest change in my life. I now work in a classroom of forty children and four adults. We share the children, and all of us show ownership. We celebrate their diversity because we celebrate and model our own. Our teaching, our caring, our learning, our inspirations have reached new levels. Now it is easy to focus on the needs of each child, and to facilitate their growth. This support has let me know I made the right choice for me— teaching. I think all of us dread a return to teaching alone.

Third-grade teacher, New York

Inclusion is one of the most rewarding things I do, when appropriate, and one of the most frustrating, when not appropriate. Last year I had a wonderful little boy who had autism, and working with him was a joy. His TSSs (technical support staff) made it that way. They worked with me, and were able to keep him focused, but also let him go when he needed it. We had a wonderful time. This year I have a Down's syndrome child who is a *major* behavior problem, extremely disruptive. The TSS is not very good with him, and does not use the suggestions I give. I have had him two years now; last year inclusion was just for play, this year is full-time. The TSS is the key to good inclusion. I have no control over who the TSS is.

I have had inclusions without TSS, and if the behavior is acceptable, I individualize and include the notes of individualization on the report card, I give the same report card to all, and note modifications so the next placement is informed. That way, I try to avoid inappropriate placement, and the parents are not under the assumption that their kid is really doing kindergarten work.

Another problem is having inappropriate inclusion students. Their parents want them to be normal, so they can put them into a regular classroom when it is not the best place for the child or the rest of the class. On top of that, add an aide, or TSS, who doesn't follow through, or is not consistent with the behavior plan. One year I had a child with Down's syndrome who was mainstreamed full-time into my afternoon kindergarten, with twenty-five other kids, and no other teacher or aide.

The large classes, with twenty-plus students, are the problem in every area. Individualization is too difficult to do with a class of more than twenty, even if there are just the regular everyday behavior problems.

Kindergarten teacher, Pennsylvania

Multiple concerns in middle and high school

Middle and high school teachers face concerns that are distinct from those confronting their elementary school colleagues. Their students have different teachers for a shorter amount of time throughout the day. They are expanding their sphere of influence beyond family and school as they assert their independence from parents and other grown-ups. Many have jobs that take up most of their time out of school, leaving minimal time for homework. Peers offer friendship, validation, and pressure as teenagers establish their own identity.

The most stressful situation in which I find myself as a teacher is when I come to the realization that a student is involved in drugs or alcohol, which, unfortunately, happens quite often. I keep an open classroom and make myself available to the students both before and after school to discuss any problems or concerns they might have. The problem is, I have to wait for them to come to me. I can address the issue if the student comes to school high or drunk, but, quite often, I find the information out when they seek me out to talk. I have had extensive training regarding drug and alcohol prevention and intervention, but the bottom line is that each student must make his or her own decision.

Middle school teacher, New York

I think being a first-year teacher has some stress built right in. I am currently preparing for three different types of math classes, as well as coteaching with a special education teacher. There are a few areas of teaching that probably stand out to me as the most stressful. First, the high population of ESL students: I have twenty-nine students in a low math course, and only about two-thirds speak English. Mixed in with the language differences, I have a huge range of abilities. I try to make my lessons shorter in that class, so I have ten or fifteen minutes to walk around and give extra help to those who need it. I also have started an after school study group that meets on Thursdays. Although I had the students take home a note that was signed saying I strongly recommend their son/daughter to stay after to get the extra help, only a third of them show up each Thursday. The second most stressful situation I am dealing with is the behavior problems in one of my classes. I have four fifteen-year-old eighth graders who are repeating a grade. Out of the four, only one is passing. It is extremely frustrating that these kids are allowed to sit in my class, make constant disruptions and threats to me, and do absolutely nothing, so the result is that they fail again. I feel as though these kids are wasting a whole year of their life, ruining my class for my other twenty-five students, and making my life more stressful than it needs to be. One of those students has a parole officer, has been suspended *many* times, has made threats to me and other teachers, had a court date two weeks ago for assaulting a teacher at this school, is failing my class with 2.3 percent, etc. Obviously this school is not the best place for this student to be, and even though he makes me crazy every day, I still go home each night and try to figure out what I can do to help him. I wake up thinking about him and how sad his situation is, and yet I even have a little bit of fear of him. He is just an insecure, macho fifteen-year-old boy, and yet I don't know how far his temper would push him.

Middle school teacher, Virginia

The following teacher faces a different set of stresses in a college preparatory school.

My students are among the most stressed in the world, I think. Our school is an all-girls, college-prep, Catholic school, and there is much competition and concern about grades. One of the ways I try to help them is to talk with them about their workload and expectations. I always emphasize that grades don't really matter in the long run, that what is learned is what counts, but their realities are different. Sometimes, I make sure that we start class with prayer or meditation to calm them down, if they seem really upset. They really like visualization and meditation as ways to cope with stress, but we have found through surveys that they don't use those techniques at home. Our students usually respond to stress in un-healthy ways, and we try to model good techniques in the class-room. I even taught one of my classes how to knit, ostensibly for the history content, but also to help with stress.

High school teacher, Ohio

Many teachers are continually thinking of new ways to help the children entrusted to them.

I am going back to school to get my second master's degree. This one is in Art Therapy and Counseling. I have found that it is no longer enough to be able to teach them to read; now I have to be able to get them to a place where they are able to learn. My art making has helped me through so much (divorce, death of a parent, empty nest, etc.) that I have found myself trying to use it more and more with my students. The courses also help me with the understanding and tech-nique necessary to help my students with their coping problems. Every year there seems to be a theme in the problems that come my way in the classroom, and this year it is the year of the abused child. Art therapy is the path that seems to provide me with the feeling that I am becoming more competent to meet my students needs

First-grade teacher, Illinois

Parents

Parents and other primary caregivers including grandparents, aunts and uncles, older siblings and foster parents affect the teaching and learning experience in school. In the best circumstances, they provide support and partnership. Parents can also undermine the teacher's goals and the student's progress, both through their lack of involve-ment and their excessive preoccupation in their children's educational lives. How parents respond to specific aspects of school greatly effects the teaching and learning fabric in a classroom, school, and school sys-tem. One missed stitch can unravel the entire piece.

Teacher-parent relationships

In elementary schools, teacher-parent relationships are an essential component in children's learning. Most teachers have several parent conferences a year, and frequently see parents at school when they come in to help or pick up their children at the end of the day. Teachers take these relationships seriously and work diligently to keep them professional and yet friendly. Regardless, working with parents takes time and energy and the experiences can be both joyful and stressful, as exemplified in the following comments.

The first and I think most powerful thought that comes to mind as a teacher is the fragile relationship we have with parents. I always worked hard at creating a safe, open, welcoming community . . . a home away from home. It was always delightful in working with the children, as they are always so open and willing to share. It was always so stressful, for me as a teacher, when I acquired information that I was uncomfortable with, either through something a child disclosed or a parent shared with me. I think in our practice we open ourselves to establishing "community," creating an extended family . . . sometimes within those safe parameters we establish, people feel comfortable enough to share *all* of their stuff. The issue here is that it is not always what the kids share, but when parents begin to tell you frankly how they discipline their child, how they handle homework, what is going on between them and their spouse, etc., the lines become rather fuzzy. I have always appreciated the openness people have brought into my classroom. I think any little piece of the puzzle just helps me be aware and relate better to that particular child and what is going on for them. Yet we walk a fine line when it comes to telling a parent that, in our opinion (be it professionally or just morally), we disagree with their approach to discipline or whatever. We have a very intimate view into the soul of the family. The challenge lies in what we see, what we choose not to see, and how we deal with the information we acquire to best support our children.

Preschool teacher, Ohio

My most difficult stress is dealing with a parent population who have themselves been hurt through their education and who, because of the hurt, are unwilling or unable to offer the support their students need.

Kindergarten teacher, Nebraska

43

Parents are a stress. Many parents are well-meaning but others do not respect the teaching profession. It is almost scary not knowing if what you say in class is going to be misconstrued at the dinner table. I think it boils down to a lack of respect for the teaching profession.

Kindergarten teacher, California

Consistent attendance

Consistent attendance is essential for the learning of individual students and for developing and maintaining a positive classroom community.

I have many parents who get their children to school two or three days a week in a good week and make excuses for the rest of the time. Some get their children to school every day but thirty-five to ninety-five minutes late consistently, and each year I have at least one who comes mostly after lunch.

Preschool teacher, Ohio

Many teachers devote a great deal of their time helping parents to understand the importance of consistent attendance. One year I had a student who consistently came in after we had started group. While we were singing and reading big books, she was putting away her coat. She had missed settling in with her friends and getting her writing materials ready for writer's workshop. Each day that she was late, she would start on the margins of our community and behind in her school work, and would spend the rest of the day trying to catch up. I worked with her mother throughout the year to help her see the importance of having her daughter enter the classroom with her peers.

When a child is consistently late or absent I go through all the bureaucratic stuff I'm required to do, knowing that it will have no effect. But I call the parent or go to the house if there is no phone. I appeal to the parent's wishes for their child to do well in life and explain what he or she is missing both academically and socially. I also ask if there is any way I can help. I have found two situations that I have been able to help. And once so far just the talk with the parent brought an immediate change in the attendance.

Preschool teacher, Ohio

Teachers continually work to understand their students' particular learning styles and to develop specific ways to teach them. This individualized approach is undermined by excessive absences and inconsistent attendance of their students.

> I individualize everything we do but find I am not getting to some children as often as I want. Some have such erratic attendance that I seem to just get ahold of what they need and find they are absent again for a few days.
>
> *Elementary teacher, Oregon*

Homework support

Students need appropriate support from home with their homework. This support includes help with the work itself, but also help in having a quiet place where they can do the homework and keep their supplies and book bag. Each year I seem to have several students whose parents don't look at the homework and don't help their children find lost school books.

> *Elementary teacher, Arizona*

When parents and teachers work together and communicate honestly about the intellectual, social, and emotional well-being of their students, learning is enhanced, self-esteem increases, and the classroom atmosphere becomes stress-free. With the current emphasis nationwide on educational standards and high-stakes testing, this collaboration is essential if we want students to be proficient readers and writers and caring human beings.

5

Standards and Testing

STANDARDS AND testing have become an integral part of the lives of teachers in the past five years. When I retired from the classroom in 1994, very few people were even mentioning them. As I write, forty-nine states have standards and many have accompanying testing that each school system must administer. State and school system standards and testing varies greatly from state to state and school system to school system. Whenever I meet with teachers, however, the issue of standards and testing permeates the conversation.

I received more e-mail responses on this topic than to any other question, and from the correspondence, it is apparent that the topic is extremely complicated. As we have seen in Chapter 2, teachers have high standards for their students, and work hard to create optimum teaching opportunities. Most teachers believe that they can best help their students move forward by creating and administering their own observation and assessment (testing) measures. Some are comfortable with standards that focus on attitudes of learning and some believe that their particular school system would benefit from consistent standards and expectations. The difficulties arise when they are required to teach specific information with a particular methodology as part of the expectation that all their students will master the grade level body of knowledge.

Most of the teachers who e-mailed me were in general agreement about the ways that standards and testing affected the teaching and learning in their particular classrooms:

- Tests and results do not represent what the children know and have learned.
- The accompanying pressures that teachers, students, and parents feel are negative to self-esteem.
- The political use of testing results undermines their benefits.
- There are significant equity issues that need to be addressed.
- The current focus on state standards and testing has undermined teachers' professionalism.
- The emphasis on standards and testing has resulted in curriculum imbalances and curriculum that is not developmentally appropriate.

In response to my letter on standards and testing, I heard from a predominance of kindergarten teachers. A great deal of what the kindergarten child is learning is developmental and can't be "taught" or tested in a paper and pencil way. Kindergarten teachers are being required to give up some of the physical activities—music, art, block building, and developmental play—that they know are essential for a child's intellectual, physical, emotional, and social success.

I also heard from a predominance of California teachers on this issue. This is due in part to the fact that my letters were listed on CateNet, but may also reflect the possibility that California teachers have been required to conform to a more narrow definition and methodology of teaching literacy.

The first section of this chapter offers teachers' general reactions to how standards and testing creates stress for them and their students (see Appendix, Letter 3). The second section gives representative responses by elementary teachers to a series of questions about standards and testing (see Appendix, Letter 8). In the third section, middle and high school teachers express some of their concerns about the effects of standards and testing on their student population.

Teacher Stress, Standards, and Testing

As far as the standards movement, I appreciate that we, as educators, must hold students to high standards. However, in California the standards are not standards—they are specific, detailed, grade-level expectations for literacy and mathematics achievement. Standards are supposed to be general, broadband types of norms for student achievement whose variables would include the *time* it takes to achieve those standards! In other words, they should take into account that not every child will achieve these standards at the same time—that *time* is the variable, not the standard itself. Also, the way in which the standards were instituted in our state gave no phasing-in time. The standards were simply created and adopted and they are expected of all students in the state. A much more reasonable approach would have been to say that, for instance, the kindergarten students starting in the 1998 school year will be responsible for those standards as they progress in school and, at the end of their high school career, will have to pass an exit exam in order to receive a diploma. Instead, the governor is mandating a high school exit exam that must be passed by all high school students starting in the class of the year 2004. It is sheer madness to expect our students to master this exam without the benefit of trained teachers' instruction at "standards levels" for their entire school career. There have been no concerted efforts to train teachers statewide about standards-based teaching and instruction. That is not to say that teachers are not trying to meet this challenge, but given the enormity and complexity of the educational legislation that has passed in recent years, it will take us years to even reach the levels of professional development needed for such a daunting task! Let alone the fact that mandated class size reduction (now in its fourth year of implementation) requires an increasingly larger number of teaching professionals each year!

First-grade teacher, California

This is one subject that hit very close to home with me at this particular time. You see, I am an educator in California and we have been under fire from politicians and the state governors for two terms now and I'm a bit battle-weary. First of all, let me say that I am not anti-standards or anti–standardized testing, but I have a *big* problem when that test is held over our collective heads as a means of financial incentives. I object wholeheartedly to monetary rewards or sanctions relying on test scores because we have *no* control over the students who are entrusted to our care! Both the previous governor, and now our current governor, have proposed and instituted these kinds of competitive programs in our state.

First-grade teacher, California

I consider myself to be one of the few remaining whole language teachers, and what I keep reminding myself, as well as my colleagues, is that good teaching is what counts the most. My students do well and I avoid putting any emphasis on the tests or their scores. It's getting harder and harder as the media continues to barrage the public with the importance of raising test scores and *how* it should be done. I often feel as though I'm fighting a losing battle. Standardized testing reinforces the traditional model of teaching that makes my job even harder because I have to defend my philosophy of teaching all the time. It undermines my efforts to get my kids to think about how they can get an answer, see multiple solutions, explain their thinking. I also see that teacher education is only supported if it boasts the ability to raise scores. It seems to me like standardized testing and standards are taking the heart out of teaching.

Multiage primary teacher, California

I am so tired and overwhelmed right now I don't think I could even think about taking a graduate school class. The state increased its demands on schools and teachers. Forty percent of our teachers lack credentials and go to school at night, and now we have lost our staff development days, which we had been using as time for scoring performance-based assessments.

Elementary literacy teacher, California

Because there is so much pressure on teachers to raise test scores excessive class time is spent practicing filling in bubbles and learning the format of the tests. I recently heard of a teacher who worked at a CA school where it was mandated that they spend ONE HOUR A DAY practicing for the test, starting now!

Multiage primary teacher, California

Politics and the policies being put into place that affect our classrooms seem to be the most stressful thing to me. It is very frustrating to be part of such a knowledgeable group of professionals who get little respect from the policymakers at the state or federal level. This coming week is testing week and these tests force us to prepare kids in ways that are developmentally inappropriate. So, my main stress comes from those mandates from above that I know are not right for my students and that I cannot control/change.

Fourth-grade teacher, Ohio

The tests disrupt everything we have been doing. The learning becomes disjointed as I try to introduce things that are not covered in the regular curriculum in the two weeks prior to testing. The test is administered to half the class at a time while the other half sits uncomfortably in the cafeteria watching videotaped cartoons. Those students who do not sit quiet and still are made to stand in the back of the cafeteria touching their toes until it is time to go back to their class. This goes on for four consecutive mornings if there are no absences. If I do have to do some makeup testing due to absences, it continues for a fifth day. During this time there are no art or gym classes. Afternoons are difficult because the routine has been disrupted and they have had to sit so still for a whole morning that we need to do a lot of activities that require movement. I really feel the whole situation (the tests themselves, the long hours of inactivity, the punishment for not being still) is abusive to the children.

Kindergarten teacher, Michigan

The results of the new standards tests have created havoc in my school. I have never seen such stress. My school has now taken library away from teachers as a prep time. During this time teachers now take low children and work with them. Fourth-grade chorus is now only for those who are not low academically because they are now taken out of chorus and given tutoring time. Recess is no longer recess if you are low—you are kept in up to three times a week for tutoring. Morale is really low and I wonder if it is only my school.

Kindergarten teacher, New York

What has happened is that no one "in authority" seems to understand that while they are raising their expectations in the testing situation, in reality we are finding that the students that we are trying to teach are more and more disturbed, less able to learn, parents are using more drugs and alcohol than ever before and therefore providing less and less support and supervision in the home.

First-grade teacher, Illinois

The direction the state is going on mandating assessments is most stressful. We need to be accountable; however, it seems to me the state doesn't quite understand what goes on in the classroom. They don't understand most teachers are quite dedicated to their profession and spend countless hours on their curriculum. I would like the state to have many teachers from all different areas of California in all sorts of grade levels participate in the decision making process.

Kindergarten teacher, California

The standards and standardized test mania is ruining my local school system. Just five years ago I would have gone to bat against anyone choosing a private school around here and now I cannot, in good conscience, recommend my local public school. The tests and standards are draining creativity and innovation out of the classroom. I see *lots* of fill-in-the-bubble work and less and less that requires actual thought. Teachers are stressed more than ever to "cover" what they are supposed to which results in spending relatively short amounts of time covering a lot of different things . . . and nothing very well. I am discouraged and disgusted and if I had the money I would put my kids in private school. I *never* would have said that five years ago. Frustrated and disheartened in CA.

Elementary teacher, California

In my school we all feel the stress as the MCAS testing dates loom on the horizon. The fourth-grade teachers feel it the most, as if the success of their students depended solely on them. But the stress is there for all of us, even those of us in kindergarten.

Kindergarten teacher, Massachusetts

Questions and Responses to the Effects of Standards and Testing

In one letter I asked specific questions about standards and testing. In attempting to keep the questions open-ended and not lead teachers to answer in a particular way, I wrote them as yes or no questions and asked the teachers to elaborate. The responses in this section are with a few exceptions from elementary teachers.

Do the standards and tests represent what your students know and have learned?

In general, the standards are far above where the majority of students are working. The idea is to *raise* the bar, so current student performance was not to be an influence. I probably haven't given them a hard enough look to say. I have been busier teaching children than standards.

First-grade teacher, California

The tests often do not show what the kids know because of the nature of the questions and the scoring. As far as our norm-referenced, multiple-choice tests go, they seem to try to trick the kids. Usually when I talk to kids, I find that their incorrect answers sometime make more sense than the "test correct" answer. I think it is hard to determine if the tests show what the kids know because teachers never really get to see the tests. It is hard to determine a kid's strengths and weaknesses based on a numerical printout of percentiles and stanines. Our state proficiency test is more open-ended, but again it is such a "secret test" that teachers are not even allowed to look at it. The standards for the test are very high and the state is starting a "reading guarantee"—students who do not pass the test in fourth grade will be retained.

Third-grade teacher, Ohio

It depends on the population of students and the district I have worked in. I have taught in seven schools (one was private), in five districts, with white rural students, white and Hispanic rural students, black and Hispanic inner-city students, and white suburban students. I think they have been closer aligned with my white, middle-class students (both rural and suburban). However, I do not believe the standards and tests represent the Hispanic students I have worked with in Colorado or the inner-city Hispanic and black students I have worked with in Nevada.

High school teacher, Nevada

I have assessment portfolios with work samples collected over the course of the year. If every teacher did this, and the state accepted this as valid assessment, a lot of the pressure would be removed. I also don't like how the state standards and tests have begun to dictate the curriculum and the adopted programs we are required to use. The kids' needs would be better served if teachers were allowed more discretion in choosing appropriate materials to get their kids up to the standards. This would be helpful even if the tests remain in use.

Fourth-grade teacher, Oregon

Are the standards and tests developmentally appropriate for your students?

As far as my comments about the kindergarten students, that is what the state standards and the "phonics is the only way to teach reading" people have wrought upon our five-year-olds. Our district has set a reading criteria for these same kindergarten students—to earn a promotion to first grade they must read at a level four (Reading Recovery level). As an experienced kindergarten teacher, it breaks my heart to see total and utter disregard for the developmental aspects of how young children acquire and learn literacy. There is an (unrealistic) assumption that all children will come to school ready to learn, but this simply is not the case, especially in the area where I live and teach—high poverty, low parental literacy, and many second language learners. I know that this is the reality in many California communities and beyond!

Kindergarten teacher, California

What I dislike the most about our State Standards is that they have been pushed down from above so that we are asking our young children to master skills before they are developmentally ready to handle them. A recent article in our local paper quoted several "experts" in the area of math saying that we should be going back to the drill and skill approach and abandon the hands-on, manipulative programs. These experts have probably never heard of Piaget or any brain research on how young children learn. There is also so much material expected to be covered that there is little time for allowing children to make discoveries. It is so much faster for the teacher to stand up in front and tell the students how to find answers that I'm afraid many will abandon any approach that lets the students problem solve. I see that a lot of material will be covered with little regard for going in-depth or striving for understanding on any concept. Then we are asked to assess how they are learning with a standardized norm-referenced test. The information attained by examining these test scores in useless for guiding instruction or measuring student progress. It feels like we are going backwards in educating our students. Back to where we only care if kids can regurgitate facts and right answers.

Multiage primary teacher, California

My district is completing its own standards, which are more commonsense. Yet I see that we will align more to the state in the near future. With the threat of reviews, raises and re-hiring attached to scores, it really chokes up those of us with the little ones who are so developmentally diverse in their progress. In my school the classes are decided by parent requests, not by heterogeneous mixing. Certain teachers also are given certain types of kids. Some teachers are more developmental (child-centered) in their approach and tend to get the kids that need some "extra" time to develop at their own rate while others may get the high achievers (or perhaps they should be called "Good Test Takers") because their rooms are more traditional (assessment-centered) and the developmental needs of the others wouldn't be well-tolerated. I am filled with fear and trepidation we'll see more and more of those "traditional" (rows and round robins) rooms as the standards are held to something so tangible as a teacher's position.

First-grade teacher, California

We are no longer able to accept developmental differences as such, because state testing does not allow for it. It has gotten out of control. I used to love to teach. Now I just feel inadequate most of the time. One person just can't do what is needed to be done. I think it is worse for more experienced teachers, because you know what needs to be done but is not being done.

First-grade teacher, California

The standard, as I see it, is a goal. It is what we want of our best students. Therefore, developmentally the standard may be unattainable at the moment for some students.

Second-grade teacher, Indiana

There is subtle pressure from the administration not to take the kids out for recess. Now, can you imagine keeping a group of five year olds inside all day? So I take my class outside and call it gross motor planning as part of PE.

Kindergarten teacher, Massachusetts

At the kindergarten level, the standards only create stress when I feel that they are developmentally beyond my student's ability to grasp. For instance, we have one hundred words that each kindergartner is supposed to know in isolation. No one decided which one hundred words a two-year-old is supposed to be able to say. We are simply delighted that they can speak at all.

Kindergarten teacher, Indiana

Questions such as "Which man lived closer to our time? Abraham Lincoln, Martin Luther King, or Christopher Columbus?" do nothing to test the ability of my first graders to think, learn, and make sense of the world. It only tests if the teacher has taught that particular lesson in such a way that it remains important in the children's memory. Not a question of major developmental understanding, but one that most kids get right because they have usually done something for Martin Luther King Day, and they remember the name.

First-grade teacher, Indiana

I did have an awful experience with testing when my principal at the elementary school where I was teaching first grade lost his job because our test scores didn't improve fast enough. Our school was devastated, as this gentleman is probably the finest principal that most of the teachers had ever worked with. That was stressful for everyone, including the students. I left that school because the new principal had us teaching the test all day long—that was all we did. The kids "practiced" all day. There was no teaching going on and I became frustrated. Every time I turned around, there was another box of pretests or posttests to give along with thousands of worksheets! Being a hands-on kind of person, I really resented using these worksheets with six-year-olds. It was all so developmentally inappropriate. So, I changed jobs and went to the high school.

First-grade teacher, Texas

I seesaw between teaching what I am told to teach and trying to teach what the children need or are ready to learn. I make more time for reading and writing and thoughtful discussion and then find that I have left out some important part of the curriculum. Then I get really stressed and try to fit it all in along with the necessary role-playing and discussion about community and behavior.

Kindergarten teacher, Michigan

The first-grade curriculum has essentially been moved down to kindergarten. One of the problems is that in our school system there is funding available only for half-day programs and we're suppose fit a full day's teaching into a half-day program. It's really difficult teaching all that I have to teach, keeping it developmentally appropriate, and still trying to find time to do all the fun kindergarten stuff that is essential for the children's development as whole people. So I feel stressed, and do a balancing act, trying to fit everything in at least three times a week.

Kindergarten teacher, Oregon

In Ohio, we have fourth grade proficiency tests and from kindergarten on you are pushed to do your part in getting them ready to pass those tests. This causes a lot of stress for both students and teachers.

First-grade teacher, Ohio

Having taught fourth grade for a while (the grade in which kids have very high-stakes test in Ohio), I feel that the test is appropriate for ten-year-olds. I think kids are ready to take a test at that age. However, what the legislature is doing with the test is totally inappropriate for children of this age. Initially, the test was designed to identify kids who we might need to keep an eye on in middle/high school—make sure we give them enough support. Now, the standards have been raised and children will be retained, etc. if they fail. It is not the test so much that is the problem, but the high stakes associated with them. When tests were low key, the kids didn't seem to have a problem. They were just a small waste of time.

Fourth-grade teacher, Ohio

Do standards and tests support your curriculum?

Here in Texas, we don't count on our curriculum to make sure that our students are ready for the test, we use the test as the curriculum!

High school teacher, Texas

An amusing question since we are pretty much writing our curriculum to support the test. Interestingly, curriculum has become secondary. If it isn't in the test, it isn't valued. Most schools in the state have had to rewrite curriculum to match the test. This was a goal of the state to begin with. Make us accountable. We, first- and second-grade teachers, have now been given the daunting task of completing about two hours of formal assessment on every child that has a certain report card performance in any of five areas. Over a half hour of the assessment is one-on-one. When I worked on the committee planning this assessment I was reassured that reading teachers would be giving the assessments to insure objectivity and alleviate teacher pressure. Today somehow the curriculum administrator got my entire grade level to agree to do all the assessment in their own classrooms. It is assessment for data and not what I would use to drive instruction. I am feeling an overriding sense that I better well cover myself and test all students (and not just those meeting the report card criteria) "just in case." We have just been told about it today (January 5), and it all needs to be done by January 31.

First-grade teacher, California

Now I live in Texas, where the teachers teach the test all year long. Students practice the test all year. I'm not sure that there is much teaching of content in many classrooms. With so much pressure on test scores, teachers have been forced to spend much of their classroom instructional time giving pre- and posttests to make sure that the students will be ready for the big tests. I just don't think that there is much teaching and learning going on between the pre- and posttests! They are simply giving more practice tests as "instructional time."

High school teacher, Texas

State standards themselves are very compatible with our philosophy and curriculum in Nebraska with the exception of the isolated phonogram section, which states that by first grade children will know and use all "seventy" phonograms. No one is sure what the "seventy" are so someone started handing out a ridiculous list from an isolated, traditional phonics program and people started to panic. Things like *ough* and diphthongs are listed there. So some teachers decided that for accountability they had to make out a criterion reference list and check them off for every student. Since the standards are supposedly voluntary, most level-headed teachers have not become so frantic and are continuing to integrate the ones that are developmentally appropriate. If this stress level continues, however, I can visualize some highly frustrated early learners.

Kindergarten teacher, Nebraska

I would like to comment on our newly instituted state standards set for Wyoming. Our school district in the capitol city of Cheyenne has provided a few inservices (mandatory attendance before or after school) during the first quarter of this 99–00 school year about the importance of implementing the new standards into our curriculum and lesson plans. While many teachers moaned about the extra work it requires jotting down the numbered benchmarks into their lesson plans, most are now used to it as second semester is upon us. I for one think the standards and corresponding benchmarks are right on target for my kindergarten grade level. I immediately welcomed the organization of the set standards, and find that it makes my job easier as I plan instructional activities. I devised a weekly lesson plan template on the computer plugging in the many benchmarks that I "cover" during my classroom routine. (And I must admit it does look quite professional!) I have been using the formatted template all year, and only have to jot down the literature or math manips, etc., I use to meet the required standards/benchmarks—what a timesaver! I find the set standards to be very beneficial as it helps me to stick with activities or lessons that are purely instructional, worthy, and effective, instead of "cutesy-pooh." The new standards help me to stay focused when I plan, as I think, "What are the kids learning with this chosen activity?" I do not want to waste their time! I also like how the new standards have been matched with our new report card this school year! "Grading" is easier and more precise now that it utilizes a rubric format showing who is still working on the expectations and who has mastered it/them. I have always preferred a work-at-your-own-pace mastery-learning style for my students. Our school district has mandated that teachers post the standards around each classroom so students and *parents* are clear about the expectations for each grade level. Some of my classroom parents have asked for copies of the state standards to take home to better help their children "make the grade." Parents have told me they like the new easy-to-read kindergarten "curriculum." I realize my enthusiasm for the newly set standards is not shared with all my colleagues inside this school district, or even at this one small school of three-hundred students. And for my grade level, there aren't any formal "testing" procedures as there are for all other grades. So, maybe I am more comfortable because of that?

Kindergarten teacher, Wyoming

We had the Metropolitan Achievement Test two weeks after February break. The stress it creates is mostly due to its lack of relationship to our regular curriculum. It covers math, science, and reading. We are required by the administrators to include minilessons in our daily lesson plans for the two weeks prior to the test teaching what the children need to know for the test. (Our lesson plans are checked every week throughout the year by an administrator.) So lessons become pretty disjointed as we try at least to introduce the words and concepts in the science part of the test. The reading part is difficult for even our best readers and the questions are all inferential. So we feel like somehow we haven't done our job even though we know the progress our children have made over the year. Some teachers try to introduce some background information to help the children read at least the first two passages—one is on Peru and the other on pandas.

Kindergarten teacher, Michigan

From my perspective working at a regional educational lab serving states with strong standards movements, I see a real mix of attitudes and outcomes. Most teachers see the value of identifying common goals and improving teaching practices around them. However, the burden of added assessments is stressful, especially if they don't naturally fit into and guide instruction.

High school teacher, California

The major stress in my teaching situation is the Stanford Achievement Test. There is so much pressure on the teachers and principals to do well on this test. I am not sure where you live and if your school system is in the same situation as ours so I will not elaborate on this topic, which it itself alone could be a book. To relieve this stress I have to just tell myself that I am doing my best. I teach the course-required objectives and do so in a manner that motivates my children to learn.

Third-grade teacher, Alabama

I seem to do more testing than teaching these days.

Fourth-grade teacher, Massachusetts

Are you able to use the testing results for diagnostic purposes?

One of the appeals of the performance-based testing to our district is that it does offer us another view of our students. I don't mind the test so much as what they do with it. I think it keeps us aware when we see how we rank with other districts in general achievement. We do our students a disservice to make them feel they are up there with the average population in all ways when they aren't. I am reminded of an anecdote from Martin Luther King Jr.'s passage from high school to college. He had been an honor student in his high school, but needed remediation to keep up in college. He was able to catch up to his peers, but the blow from not even knowing he was behind was a powerful one, and spoke volumes about lowered expectations in some schools, particularly a black school in his case. But the same test results are not helpful for individual students' instruction.

Curriculum coordinator, California

The state thinks these results can be used, but again it is *very* difficult to make instructional decisions without seeing a child's actual work. With scores, stanines, etc., it makes no sense. We can see their strengths and weaknesses, but not enough to make instructional decisions. If "comprehension" is a weakness, that is just not enough to tell us what the child is doing so we can help.

Third-grade teacher, Ohio

At present I am working with a small group of teachers in our building to develop standards for reading and writing, complete with rubrics. This work is new for us and we are just beginning to understand what that might look like. We are trying to design performance tasks around the standards that will tell students exactly what we feel good quality work is. We are hoping that the performances of understanding will enable parents and others to know and understand what it is that we expect of our best students at each grade level. The performance tasks will then become part of each student's portfolio.

Second-grade teacher, Indiana

There is a trend among the big administrators to recognize accountability only through quantifiable data. But I just think of Einstein, who said "Everything that counts can't be counted and everything that is counted doesn't necessarily count."

Elementary teacher, South Dakota

Our state test is *very* difficult, but I don't know if equity is an issue. We aren't allowed to see it ever. The state just decided to sell copies of old tests, so we will finally be able to see what our kids have been asked to do for the past seven years.

First-grade teacher, California

In regard to your school system's economic position, has testing influenced you and your students?

Our particular school has kept up with the suburban schools in the past on tests. But presently there is a big debate in our school about the kinds of kids we accept for entrance into our all-city magnet program. We get kids by lottery. Any child can come. But some teachers want to put a stipulation on which kids we accept. It seems that we are beginning to get students who "need to be taught." Ha! Some teachers want to mandate parental involvement before the parents sign up for our magnet. They also want prospective middle school students to write some kind of entrance paper to be accepted. My thinking is that any kind of requirement put on parents to get their child into our school will automatically weed out the lowest and poorest students. I don't think this would be an issue if the stakes weren't so high with standardized testing. I think some of our teachers get a little anxious around test time because now we can receive merit pay. Last year each teacher in our building received $900 dollars extra in salary because of our scores (about $572 after taxes ate its share). I don't think this is fair. I feel like I had a much harder job at my previous building where all of my students ate free lunch, came to school two to three years behind in vocabulary development, and thus qualified for my Chapter I all-day kindergarten. Yet my previous colleagues did not get this extra salary.

Second-grade teacher, Indiana

Do you see any equity issues that need to be addressed?

This is my current worry about the standards: achieving them at Chapter I schools. Last year while on special assignment in support of other teachers, I worked at Chapter I schools where teachers were working like dogs to define curriculum to meet standards and to make that curriculum meaningful *and* rigorous for their students. I do not see the standards making their jobs any easier. Their jobs are indeed the most challenging, and the standards have only defined how far their students must go . . . when they are so behind already. Burnout at these sites is clearly apparent this year, where teachers feel overwhelmed with the standards because they are so far away from meeting them, which is so clearly the goal.

First-grade teacher, California

Yes! We are a large, poor, urban system surrounded by wealthier high-scoring suburban systems. When I began teaching in '74 we had the highest teaching salaries in the county. We attracted the best teachers. Now, because of mandated busing, our system has been raped of many of the best teachers and principals, and we have the lowest salaries. The suburban schools that took our students got double tuition because of desegregation. (They figured it took more money to educate these urban students.) Their students attend newly-built schools and have the newest technology equipment in labs and classrooms, along with many of our best teachers.

Second-grade teacher, Indiana

I am an expert in the field of second language learners and do believe that they are receiving short shrift in this high-stakes standards and testing fiasco! First of all, what happened to multiple measures? No one, and I mean *no one, adult or child,* should be evaluated on one measure, namely a standardized test given once a year! We currently have a state program of school improvement that utilizes this test as its only academic measure. While standardized tests have their worth, it is my belief that this worth is to compare general knowledge for a relatively small, narrow band of students. We can't use one measure to compare *all* students when dealing with the extreme diversity we have in California. Secondly, we must deal with the cultural biases that exist in standardized tests. Many of our current students are not prepared to take these tests in the multiple-choice format. If they have been schooled in another country for part of their educational history, they may never have encountered this format before. For instance, in Mexico, many of the year-end exams are given orally and the students are expected to answer questions in front of the entire class. Written essays are also a part of their year-end evaluations, not a multiple-choice, fill-in-the-bubble type of test. These students are not used to this type of test format, let alone the idea that it should be the only measure of how well they are doing in a particular class or grade level. Thirdly, I have a problem with tests that are normed with student populations very unlike our multicultural and ethnic realities in California. Don't even get me started on the validity of giving this one-size-fits-all test to students whose first language is other than English and who have been in the state or country fewer than twelve months—our state *requires* them to also take this test! There should exist, at the very least, a measure of English proficiency *before* taking the state-mandated test!

Teacher of five-, six-, and seven-year-olds, California

Our district consistently scores third from the bottom in state testing. We are about 80 percent Hispanic and 80 percent free lunch. Average educational background of the adult population is probably about sixth grade, and fear of flying bullets is very real. We work hard teaching traumatized kids, and we love the work we do. Then we get ranked third from the bottom every year, but we try to ignore that and just focus on what we are doing to help kids. Sometimes their emotional needs override their need to know the multiplication tables, even though we cannot keep them out of gangs and drugs, which their families are in.

Elementary teacher, California

Our economic position is poor. Poor kids in a poorly-funded district. We continue to be poor. Most of the mandated stuff has caused some redirection of money and we do notice that there are no more field trips and fewer aides, etc. The testing further divides people based on socioeconomic and cultural levels. We have high test scores, high property values, and one of the most homogeneous communities in Los Angeles. Not that scores are the cause, but they play into the bigger picture.

First-grade teacher, California

My district is pretty affluent but the state report cards that are based on the tests at various levels is a huge media thing when they come out. This is a new thing, so the results will probably have a big effect on how levies are passed in the future. It is too early to tell right now.

High school English teacher, California

Again, that depends on the population with them being more developmentally appropriate for the white middle-class students.

Elementary teacher, Nevada

We were considered "an inadequate school" which gave us a lot of extra funding. When the students' test scores reached a certain level, we were removed from the inadequate list, which boosted the principal's career, but resulted in less funds for our school. As far as I could tell, the students' skills and abilities were the same. The school just learned how to teach the kids to take the tests better.

High school teacher, Nevada

In Colorado, the legislature has decided that all districts must raise their test scores each year by 25 percent or their accreditation and funding will be affected. We suspect this legislation will change when they realize how unrealistic, broad, and general it is. The governor is now talking about giving extra grant money to districts that score the highest and districts that improve the most.

Elementary teacher, Colorado

Have the parents of your students responded or reacted to testing?

I teach in an affluent area and parents tend to be highly educated and our test results are generally high. Some parents put all their eggs in the testing basket. Others are wise and believe the testing prep and process take away from valuable learning time.

Elementary teacher, California

I think our parents are the ones that create stress about the testing in our building. They want their children to excel, and the kids tend to feel anxiety about testing in spite of our trying to deemphasize it. We try to relax the atmosphere at school during that week, and we do not change our regular special area schedules.

Elementary teacher, California

It seems the grown-ups just want to rank them up from the earliest age possible. It reminds me of a father of a child I have right now who wanted to consider sending his bright, creative, excellent reading, yet immature child back to first grade in December because he isn't at the "top of my class." (I have quite a number of students who will most likely be identified for gifted instruction by fourth grade.) He is a darling boy who is progressing nicely through the second grade. For this father it's all his own ego, about a ranking and the college his son will get into. Little to do with his son. Perhaps that conference was just a glimpse of what was to come this year.

Second-grade teacher, Ohio

The administration sends a flyer home letting parents know the testing schedule, stressing its importance and encouraging them to make sure their students are not absent or tardy. As a result, even though I try to downplay its importance in my classroom I always have several students who are quite agitated by the lectures they have gotten at home about testing. I reassure all the children that their grades will not be affected by the test, that I expect a lot of the test to be very difficult since it is not what we have been learning in class, and that we will use it to practice how to take this kind of a test.

Kindergarten teacher, Michigan

A group of parents from an upper middle-class school in my district approached me to find out how they could get the special education magnet out of their school because it adds thirty kids (many with IQs in the 50–70 range) to their denominator and brings their proficiency rate way down. That doesn't even begin to consider the fact that the correlation between poverty and the test is .85. The governor's response to that is that he will yank accreditation on schools that don't succeed. Guess if we lose money we will have house tours to raise money, like some of the more affluent districts do. I bet a lot of people will want to see the projects where our kids live. It's a really, really sad commentary on our society.

Third-grade teacher, Colorado

Has the emphasis on standards and testing either undermined or supported your professionalism?

The state standards create an undue stress on all! So many are absurdly specific and so inconsequential to the larger picture of reading. We then have administrators confused or uneducated about standards, testing, and pedagogy, doing as they are told. My principal is showing signs of quavering and she's a strong one. She's beginning to talk out of both sides of her mouth. I don't think she even sees herself doing it. In a district "think tank" meeting a week or so ago she said she didn't care if her teachers understood the research behind the pedagogy as long as they are using it. She is willing to strip her staff of their professionalism like that.

Elementary teacher, California

I have come back from a district grade-level meeting this evening and am dumbfounded. Our curriculum administrator was going over the assessment materials that will qualify children for our new remediation program which will take kids and put them through two hours of Open Court a week, on top of their normal school week, with the hours being from 3:30–4:30. I have some new feelings about high-stakes testing after this meeting. In my opinion our remediation program has the children as the very last concern. The main concerns are high test scores and low retention numbers. The district has chosen Open Court materials, which have been presented as a sure bet to raise scores to be used with these kids who aren't meeting our "grade level standards." I use those words but what they really mean is the children who *do* meet remediation and retention policy standards. I am not upset that these children will be getting extra services, I have problems with the types of materials that will be used. At this time my district does not test K or first grade with the SAT. Because we need "standardized data" (I heard this right from the horse's mouth) for remediation and retention policies, "the district is looking into purchasing such items (those that provide standardized data) for K and first." My school is also in the middle of "program quality review" and I have three grade-level assessments that I must give my class on top of this district stuff. At least with the math portion, my grade-level partners and I were able to create/decide upon it together without outside interference as long as we assessed what was covered on the school's plan. The writing sample we need to have students do is scripted for us in a way that is totally unnatural to the way I give writing assignments in my room. Though PQR is to be agreed upon by all staff, our "essential questions" were pretty clearly foisted on us from on high. I just want to know what this all has to do with teaching and learning? The PQR results will drive teaching to some extent but not the rest. I want my children to celebrate their learning and unique talents.

Many teachers are expected to comply with curriculum standards and rubrics that they have not had a part in creating. More difficult still is the sense that the kinds of standards that administrators and politicians often promote are not developmentally appropriate or do not promote sound pedagogy. In my career (nine years), the expectations put on teachers have been leaning more and more toward teaching to the test. This undermines my professionalism by not allowing me to teach to students needs rather than the tests.

First-grade teacher, Colorado

I'm seeing way too many really good teachers on total overload, much of it due to new testing and state accountability laws. We have a new state law, the Colorado Basic Literacy Act, which requires us to monitor the progress of all K–3 kids. We have to keep track of which kids aren't meeting proficiencies through the use of a variety of tools, including a body of evidence (kind of a portfolio) and individual assessments. The bill wasn't accompanied by funding so teachers are trying to do individual pre- and postassessments on their kids and teach the other twenty-five at the same time. They are doing it before and after school, planning times.

Curriculum coordinator, California

Push to teach a program not a child: I ignore this and just hope I won't be fired. I have, when asked, written my reasons for what I do and how I assess it. I find it is important to be able to articulate my philosophy and its applications as well as to be able to explain what the program in question does or doesn't do that I feel is educationally appropriate. Working toward my master's in reading, participating in the listservs, and attending national conferences and local workshops has been beneficial.

Kindergarten teacher, Minnesota

Have you spoken out publicly about standards and testing?

Although many teachers wrote about their concerns about the ways standards and testing are being handled in their school districts and states, very few reported that they spoke out publicly about their concerns.

No. Only at district meetings, inservices, and college classes I teach.

First-grade teacher, California

Not as much as I should.

Elementary teacher, California

I recently heard of a teacher who worked at a CA school where it was mandated that they spend *one hour a day* practicing for the test, starting now! I speak up frequently at staff meetings because it seems like many teachers are getting sucked up in the fervor to raise scores this way.

Multiage elementary teacher, California

No, I am not yet ready to do this. I work hard to make sure we are teaching well and not compromising what we know is right. I am not really in a district where parents and administration would accept public opposition to these tests from teachers. I have certainly spoken out at district meetings, etc., but the state is controlling many of the tests.

Kindergarten teacher, California

I don't have any earth-shattering answers to these complex issues, but I will tell you that I talk with my colleagues, acquaintances, and friends about these topics all the time. I have gotten involved more and more in the political discussions surrounding education and I write letters to the editor and to my legislators *all* the time! I even invited my state assemblyman to accompany me on a tour of our schools recently. (He obliged; hopefully it was educational for him—he expressed great interest in the schools!) I hope that these ideas are helpful to your project, as you might be able to tell, these are issues that are close to my professional heart and soul. Thanks for listening!

Elementary teacher, California

Only on a building level.

Primary teacher, California

This year during lunch someone asked who we could write to express our professional opinion about the inappropriate developmental level of the test. We discussed writing a letter and getting signatures from not only all the first- and second-grade teachers at our school but as many others from the district as possible. But another teacher spoke up stating that at this time no one is going to listen to teachers and we better keep our mouths shut. Most agreed. I am going to write it anyway and try to get signatures.

Kindergarten teacher, Michigan

Yes, as president of our local reading council, I have spoken out and written often about the issues of standards and testing. I am part of the International Reading Association's legislative alert network. I relay the info about the issues regarding standards and testing IRA passes on in our newsletter and at our meetings. I also present situations in my classes for my students to explore the issues of testing and standards. And, in my staff development sessions in CA, I often speak out. What is amazing to me is the number of teachers who speak out in agreement with me.

Elementary teacher, Washington

Connecticut Mastery Tests in grades four, six, and eight are resulting in more of the perennial "pushing down" of curriculum. To help me hold this at bay, I'm looking for ways to educate our decision makers so that they will understand that music, art, and physical education *are* "academics," and that playing "Duck, Duck, Goose" *is* a worthwhile way to spend some of the kindergarten school day.

Kindergarten teacher, Connecticut

My kindergarten and first-grade students must pass the Texas TAAS EXCET test in reading to graduate. When I took the job, I told my principal that yes, passing the test is important, but that more important was that my students needed to be able to read on level. I told her that if I could help my students improve their reading levels, that I knew they would pass the test. So far so good, my kids are passing and I spend a small part of my time teaching test-taking skills and most of my time teaching reading.

Kindergarten teacher, Texas

Middle School and High School

I have included two rather lengthy comments from three middle school teachers.

I would like to begin by saying that I feel comparatively less pressure from standardized testing in a private school than my friends feel as teachers in public schools. That, however, does not mean that the testing does not affect us. We participate in the IOWA exams and find that our students loathe them. Their scores generally reflect their scholastic abilities with the exception of the few students who "don't test well."

Our juniors and seniors feel the most pressure from standardized tests as they prepare for the PSATs and SATs and in some cases the ACTs. Our ESL students by far have the hardest time taking these tests for various reasons including language barriers and lack of historical knowledge with regard to the so-called American perspective.

Insofar as dealing with the stress and pressure, I find that our students generally resign themselves to the fact that they must face the inevitable and suffer through the tests. They do take prep courses such as Kaplan and Princeton Review, but they do that on their own, outside of school requirements. In addition, several of the teachers in this school like to teach test-taking skills throughout the year to help students learn the most beneficial styles of test taking. I find that the students who feel the most prepared and remain the calmest are best able to excel on the exams in relation to their own abilities. That does not mean, however, that the calmest, most focused students get the best grades, but rather that they feel that insofar as their own academic abilities go, they have succeeded above and beyond their self-expectations.

Middle school teacher, New York

As a seventh-grade language arts teacher I feel that the state standards are a good idea. However, I disagree with how they are being used.

1. The information is *not* diagnostic. My students will be tested in March and receive a number score in October which will label/peg them for life. If they wish to assess seventh grade, this should be done as an exit from the grade in late May. The students are expected to perform as though they had completed the grade and in truth they are only at about six-and-a-half grade rather than seventh grade. These students will not take the test again until tenth grade. No one will be able to pull out a sheet where the data is analyzed and begin to prescribe a program to strengthen any student's weak areas.

2. The test is much too long. The millions spent giving this test and paying graders to score this could be spent on programs for the schools.

3. The writing test tests *vocabulary!* The vocabulary passages are very high level and if a student does not have a rich background in experiences then he or she is at a real disadvantage. A good "writer" could only be partially proficient if he or she did not know the vocabulary in these "balance" items. By balance items, I mean that they were designed to balance the numbers with multiple-choice items with the reading test. Thus, I do not think the writing score is a true assessment of a student's ability to actually *write.*

4. Materials need to be developed to help students prepare for this test. Books that do this are helpful to students to prepare for IOWA tests. They get practice in the types of questions they are expected to answer and they feel more relaxed taking the tests. This test is shrouded in mystery and they feel like pawns. They ask why they should try to do well on a test they will not

get results from until October and which will not affect their grade. "For the good of the order" does not cut it as a *viable* reason to give them the passion they need to bolt them to these test booklets for three solid mornings.

5. Parents who have cared about their student's progress from infancy are still concerned about everything their students do. Many of those who are low performers have very low skills in both reading and writing and they have had significant problems in school for years. We tried a "proficiency class" at my school and it became a behavior problem for many teachers.

6. With all the millions of dollars being spent on testing, why hasn't anyone identified the *real* problem with schools? If teachers had between twelve and fifteen students from kindergarten, we would not be in this mess with low skilled secondary students. It is not the fault of poor teaching or dumb kids. *There are too many students in classes!*

7. Teachers would love to have more training in class work. However, look at what teachers are paid—especially young teachers whose peers are averaging twenty-five to thirty-five thousand more in starting salaries and asking them to pay $100 per credit hour is a real financial impossibility. Free classes with free credits would be great. Many secondary teachers were never taught how to *teach* reading. District programs are great and I have been fortunate to get instruction that way.

8. Schools feel bullied by how the scores are being used. No one has considered ESL students who are lumped in with everyone else. Special education students who need a great deal of help in the mainstream classroom cannot receive the same help they have had to be successful on a daily basis. Their scores are lumped in as well. Shouldn't there be a separate reporting for these students?

Middle school language arts teacher, California

Conclusion

For the most part, teachers have many concerns about how standards and testing are implemented in the school, and about the effects they have on the learning and well-being of their students. Kindergarten and first-grade teachers showed the most concern about the effects of standards and testing on their students. These teachers felt that standards and testing would undermine basic understandings about how young children learn and would fundamentally affect the curriculum.

6

Searching for Balance

I'm never satisfied with what I'm doing. I feel stress when I can't say *no* and take on more than I or any other reasonable adult can handle in any one week of any one year!

Kindergarten teacher, Ecuador

Balancing school and family obligations is one of the biggest challenges teachers face. A common theme is that their work as a teacher is never done, that there is always something more that they can do to fully serve the needs of their students. I feel we have an extremely stressful profession mainly because we are unable to leave our work at work. Our work daily goes home with us and takes us well into the evening to complete. In fact, it is never done.

First-grade teacher, Ohio

WHEN THE demands at home also seem never-ending, balance between one's personal and professional life is especially difficult to attain. There never seems to be enough time.

The main stress in my personal life is having to juggle attending to my family at the same time that I attend to my professional life. This is always a conflict and a struggle. I know that to do a good job as a teacher I need to put in a lot of time, thought, and reflection into what I'm doing. I need to do a lot of reading and talking things out with colleagues and in my own head. I also need to spend quality time with my family. I guess my biggest problem is that sometimes I don't know when to stop working. One way I try to deal with this is by making sure that I spend some quality time with my daughters and husband every day. It also means that on the weekends we try to reserve at least one day to go somewhere or do something together.

Kindergarten teacher, Ecuador

Balancing family time, finding time to get business-related things accomplished, having time to be with friends, pursuing personal interests, keeping in shape with exercising—too much to do.

High school teacher, Minnesota

Balancing School and Family

Although all teachers have unique ways of responding to the specific circumstances in their lives, three themes surface as important issues in balancing school and family: being a parent, being a spouse or partner, and being part of an extended family.

Being a parent

Many teachers feel that their students get their best energy and attention and that their own children get shortchanged as far as attentiveness and quality time is concerned. When difficulties arise in their own children's lives, they often feel guilty and blame themselves.

Some of the things I do to survive is make myself walk away on the weekends. I have come to realize after four years that my family is important and I try to spend as much time with my family as I can on the weekends and not worrying as much about school. In order to do this, I have stayed and straightened up a little later on Friday instead of feeling like I need to come clean up over the weekend.

Kindergarten teacher, Washington

I have three children, ages 6, 12, and 17. So they keep me going. Aaaaaaaaaaaaah! There are many nights that I come home, rush to fix some kind of a dinner, and crash. My six-year-old made me feel so bad when he said, "Mom, do you know what bedtime story is? It's when you grab a book, and you read it to your little child!" Some nights I am so tired that it takes all of my energy just to put on pajamas.

Kindergarten teacher, Indiana

I also feel stress when I feel that I'm shortchanging my own children for my students. This is hard to deal with. The guilt is sometimes so intense that it's hard to come up with ways to balance things out.

First-grade teacher, Ecuador

I want to spend more time with my daughter. I feel *very* guilty when I drop my daughter off and she is coming down with a cold and she doesn't want mommy to go.

Middle school teacher, Minnesota

I hated leaving my five-month-old son. I was teary almost every day until about February, when I sensed we were on the way to summer vacation. Even though he was well taken care of and liked being at day care, I still felt guilty about leaving him. But, it was more than that. I *wanted* to be with him. Some days my heart literally ached to be with him. I decided that while I was teaching, all of my time home with him was *with him*—I worked after he went to bed. Some weekends I would have to work and my husband took over baby duty. I really made a commitment only to work when he was sleeping.

Second-grade teacher, Virginia

I am a mom with two boys, ages fifteen and eleven. I am always curious, and often very frustrated because I don't yell in the classroom and my words are always developmentally appropriate but when I get home I am not always the same person. Now I am never cruel or hurtful, but I have always wondered and worried that maybe I give my best to my students and then my children get stuck with the leftovers.

Preschool teacher, Ohio

I remember going back to work the day after I learned that my six-teen-year-old daughter was pregnant and looking up at the wooden teacher of the year plaque hanging on my classroom wall, along with a couple of other plaques I'd received in recognition for professional efforts. I was seized with an irresistible and very angry urge to pull the teacher of the year plaque down from the wall and smash it to smithereens. I saw it then as a symbol of an obsession to be a terrific teacher, but at the expense of family. I think the only reason I didn't do it was that I would have had to admit the feelings of guilt to others.

I still have the lesson plan suggestions I sketched out on the hospital (intensive care) record papers borrowed from the nurse during the night following my daughter's near-fatal car accident. I look at that paper now and wonder what possesses me to carry on with classroom work when faced with life-and-death situations within my own family? Do I overestimate my own importance in relation to my students?

Primary teacher, Connecticut

Unlike many other jobs, teachers cannot rearrange their schedules or complete their work at a different time so they can attend events and parent conferences at their own children's school.

Don't we all know the heart-wrenching feeling of being unable (or unwilling) to arrange for time off to escort our own children into a kindergarten classroom on the first day of school because we have to be in our own classrooms, greeting incoming students and their families . . . families joyfully taking part in one of the most impor-tant days of their lives?

Kindergarten teacher, Connecticut

Being a parent and a teacher is a very difficult conflict at times. Parent-teacher conferences are always a problem, because the times available for you to conference with your children's teachers are exactly the times you need to be available to conference with the parents of your students. Sometimes it happens that the very night of your child's choir concert is a required evening meeting at your own school. I'm not always available to attend special school functions during the day at my children's schools because I am in my own classroom, teaching.

Third-grade teacher, Ohio

For other teachers, one of the biggest stress factors in their lives is that they are not parents.

I guess the biggest stress in my personal life is an ongoing struggle with singleness, and accepting and living with that, when it's very different from what I had envisioned for my life. As far back as I can remember, I have always wanted to be a wife and mom.

Third-grade teacher, Colorado

The biggest stress factor for me is not professional at all, though I suspect my job is part of the whole matter. It is, simply, the fact that I keep putting off motherhood because of all the time I give to children, and my profession. My mother says I started to teach "too early." I don't agree. I *do* think the profession is so engrossing and so consuming, it doesn't stand in the way of motherhood, it just makes it difficult to choose. I fear losing my professional edge if I grow in personal areas.

Elementary teacher, Wyoming

Being a spouse or partner

Spouses and partners give great support to the busy teacher, but they can also be sources of stress.

I guess it is also my relationship with my husband and my children that really, really grounds me. I just love being with my family, they amaze me and inspire me. They are always so supportive of who I am and what I do. I am blessed.

Preschool teacher, Ohio

I feel I'm able to handle stress better because my spouse is also in the teaching profession and she understands what I'm dealing with. We are able to help one another talk out concerns and problems.

First-grade teacher, Ohio

79

I was married two years ago and am still adjusting my lifestyle to accommodate my marriage and husband (this is a positive stress, but a stress nonetheless).

Middle school teacher, New York

My husband of nineteen years still does not understand a lot of what goes along with my job, so that is considerable stress.

Kindergarten teacher, Pennsylvania

Conflicts with my boyfriend—I try to put them out of my mind or get the issues resolved right away so that I do not have to think about them.

Kindergarten teacher, Michigan

Teachers also work hard to find ways to alleviate their stress so that they won't have to depend too heavily on their spouses and partners to get them through difficult times. Sometimes the significant adults in teachers' lives do not understand the pressures and amount of work involved in classroom teaching, and thus are not able to give teachers the kind of support they need.

Sometimes my husband doesn't realize the stress of teaching thirteen- and fourteen-year-olds—constant disciplining and bombardment of questions. I try to deal with stresses in my personal life by taking time for myself to read, play volleyball, and get outside, basically to do things that are fun for me. Having the summer to spend with my family really helps!

Middle school teacher, Minnesota

While I was teaching, I was engaged, then married. My husband was unbelievably supportive. He was in law school, which he reports was not as stressful as teaching. My biggest challenge was finding a way to unload the stresses of my day, without asking my husband to listen to me relive every minute of my day. This took a while (about an entire year), but finally I learned to let go of at least some of the things that happened at school, and to do other things, like eat dinner, or go for a walk.

Sixth-grade teacher, Illinois

Being part of an extended family

Teachers are also involved with their extended families, which can be sources of both joy and concern. Regardless, families take time. Many teachers report that they are having to help their aging parents deal with health and financial problems. They find themselves parenting their own children as well as their own parents.

> Family concerns seem to be the biggest stresses. My husband and I are now reaching the stage where our parents' health causes us concern. My parents were both quite sick in the fall, my mother-in-law is noticeably slowing down and my father-in-law died just a few years ago. We are caught in the middle between our parents and our kids, just like the rest of our generation.
>
> *Kindergarten teacher, Canada*

> I am having some tough personal/family days right now. My mom has Alzheimer's, late stage, and my dad is finally taking her to live in a home near my brother. I am waiting to hear if he follows through and gets her there. I am the youngest and my brother has resisted all my sister and I have set up and won't even let me come visit, because I clean the (filthy) house, etc. Parenting your parents is not easy.
>
> *Kindergarten teacher, Pennsylvania*

> Family difficulties are perhaps the biggest outside strain that affects my teaching. It's hard to lay these problems aside, but it is necessary and even therapeutic to do so. Last year, when my brother was in a coma and near death, and then after he died, there were many days when I was in no condition to teach. But going to work forced me to pull myself together, and the faces of the kids, bright and sweet, refreshed me and gave me a new lease on life.
>
> *Kindergarten teacher, Oregon*

> Two school-years ago (isn't that our standard for time, school-years) my mother was going into surgery (lung cancer) on the same day my school opened. Guess where I decided I just *had* to be because incoming kindergartners and their families really need to

see the *real* teacher there on their first day? So, I was on the classroom phone, in tears, telling my mother I loved her and wishing her luck as my new students were arriving! I hid my tears and got through the day. Thank God my mom made it through the surgery.

Kindergarten teacher, Connecticut

Personal Problems

Along with balancing family life with teaching life, teachers also have personal problems that they must address. Some of the most prominent are physical and emotional problems, divorce issues, sexuality issues, and financial concerns.

Physical and emotional problems

I was having all sorts of problems emotionally in my own life, though everything was in place at home. I began counseling and went steadily for over three years. During that time I learned that many people in the helping professions come from hurtful backgrounds, and that I was not alone. Many of my colleagues were also dealing with various abuses from their childhood. I was very blessed to have a group of teachers with whom I could talk about how these anxieties affected my life, and how we needed to work them out outside school so that we could be more helpful to kids at school. I have learned to keep my personal life a higher priority than I used to; a balanced teacher is a less stressful and better teacher. I find out what *really* matters in the classroom and focus energy there, understanding that I will *never* get it *all* done and accept that. Get the important things done and you will be all right.

Staff developer, California

My biggest stress in life is my endometriosis. It's a daily reminder of my humanity, and it can cause some rather basic problems. For example, when I am in pain, it's all I can do to make it through the school day, only to go home and collapse. The pain is not the only problem associated with this condition: depression from the infertility, pain, and inability to do some things I've always been able to do before can cripple me as a teacher. I'm not always as energetic as

I think I should be. Actually, the biggest stress I face is that teachers aren't supposed to ever be sick or show any weaknesses, and I can't hide it very well when I'm hurting really badly. Why should professionals deny their humanity for 6–10 hours every day because of some artificial construct society created to make it feel better?

High school teacher, Ohio

For some, teaching helps them get away from their problems.

Personally, teaching has become a sanctuary for me during the last few years. With my husband's torturous struggle with Alzheimer's and my own battle with cancer, I found solace in my classroom. With the help of loving coworkers, I continue to find joy in working with children.

Third-grade teacher, New York

Recently, some physical problems are intruding, but I try to use my theatre background to carry on regardless—the show must go on! I can bluff—can seem energetic and enthused even when I'm not really feeling that way.

Teacher educator, California

Teachers often go to school sick because they feel so responsible and know a substitute teacher can't provide the best teaching and learning for the students.

Sometimes the school administrators don't want to spend the money on substitutes or they can't find any to hire. Then children are divided among the other teachers in the grade, disrupting the plans of colleagues and consistent learning of the students. Does illness create stress, or does stress create illness? Anyway, this is a problem that affects my teaching. True, I do have sick leave available, but I generally go to work, even when I'm not feeling well, because I don't want to lose the momentum of the activities or topics, and having a sub comes often means that the kids will just be baby-sat. I try to call subs I know who are good, but I have no guarantee that I will get them.

Kindergarten teacher, Oregon

Illness, as a kindergarten teacher! I am always catching colds. I worry that when I am out sick the children will suffer. I try to leave good lesson plans.

Kindergarten teacher, New Hampshire

We went skiing at Eastertime and I broke my tibia plateau. Now, most people I know with broken legs take about six weeks to recover, but unfortunately, due to the nature of my break I was off for the rest of the year (3 months). Fortunately, I knew the teacher who came in to replace me, and was comfortable letting her use my things. I was most concerned about a stranger going through all of my files, books, etc. Also, I felt like I had let the students and their parents down by not coming back.

Kindergarten teacher, British Columbia

Being alone

The singleness thing is always hard. I think I do handle it really well on a surface level. I have a really rich full life, lots of friends, lots of blessings, lots of interests.

Primary teacher, Colorado

Divorce

This has been some year for me with a divorce, new responsibilities at work (now doing two jobs until a promotion hopefully is arranged), and going back to school. I do have stress and have found new ways to deal with it. I listen to dolphin music at work when I can. I've taken up hiking. When I am close to nature the real world evaporates and I find myself feeling spiritual, at one with the earth. My problems become insignificant and the beauty of life becomes bold. I've also undertaken doing the weight machines at the gym. It is not as peaceful as when I am out on a hike but I can lose myself and focus on the task at hand as opposed to thinking about a million things I have to do.

Teacher educator, California

Sexuality

My personal stresses are probably my most difficult stresses, and the ones that most often bring me to a halt. I am a gay divorced father of four daughters. All of the stresses that accompany such a lifestyle, from financial woes to new dating experiences, sometimes bring me to my knees. I have learned to deal with such stresses mainly through journaling. I have discovered through my reflective journaling the strength to accept life as it is and I have even discovered personal techniques for dealing with the stress. I sometimes journal over e-mail with a trusted friend who serves as a sounding board for my reflection. I cannot truly believe I could deal with the personal stress in my life without close, trusted friends.

Primary teacher, Illinois

Our daughter who is 20 decided she is gay, and my biggest fear for her is how she will be treated by society. I think as we grapple with such personal issues in our lives, we better understand how to meet the needs of our students and we stop silencing them.

Elementary teacher, Washington

Financial concerns

The lack of serious financial remuneration creates a lot of stress. The job is very demanding, time-wise, and the pay does not reflect the high level of professional training of most teachers when compared to that of other professionals. But without teachers, the world would come to a halt. When my husband was a teacher and I stayed home with three children, our kids were among the few at their elementary school to qualify for federally subsidized school lunches. That's quite a statement about how well teachers are paid. The difficulty we are having paying for college for our children is quite a stress, but we aren't going to change professions. It would just be really great if we didn't have to be in financial straits all the time.

Kindergarten teacher, Oregon

Coping Strategies

What do teachers do to balance their personal and professional lives?

Stress builds up for me during specific times of the year: we have to write long, narrative report cards based on anecdotal notes, portfolios, and work folders. This is a monumental job and has to be completed while teaching and all other living goes on. I always experience additional stress around holidays because I have family and friends at ritual celebrations such as the Passover Seder and the Jewish New Year and Thanksgiving in the fall. The stress comes from juggling preparations with everything else I do— teach and write and consult.

The way I've learned to handle both of these situations is to start early. With report card narratives, about one month before they are due, I start writing about each student. Then each week, I add and adjust. Though this takes self-discipline, it really results in a better narrative than when I completed them during the week prior to the due date. With family holidays, we purchased a huge upright freezer, and I start cooking and baking and freezing six to eight weeks before the holiday. I've also learned to let go of some things, like buying challah and cakes rather than making them. Many guests now also bring parts of the meal, lessening my work and stress. I've come to recognize that's it's the exchanges with people around a table that are far more important than the food I serve.

Middle school teacher, Virginia

Balancing being a husband and a father as well as a teacher has been the biggest challenge of my career. Often I come home from school and I feel used up when my family needs me the most. I have struggled with this all my career and I feel that I have had varying degrees of success. There have been times when I have had to leave the schoolwork at school and simply focus on my family. I no longer feel guilty, but it was a struggle. When my children were younger I had to put limits on my evening involvement at school and my weekend involvement with schoolwork. For a time I simply wouldn't allow myself to bring home any work on weekends. There was also a period of time when I was dealing with the death of a dear friend. I found that I was able to just put school on autopilot and give everything to my friend. My students and their understanding support of me at that time really helped me to get through. I have to say that children always give me unconditional love and that has ministered to me at many stressful times in my life.

Fourth-grade teacher, Oregon

In addition to teaching school, I also teach jazzercise classes in the evenings. I think that this has a great influence over my good health. I see colleagues all around me who neglect their health because of the pressures of working with at-risk students. I teach in an area that is greatly affected by poverty and crime. In an effort to offer so much to these students some of my colleagues "give it their all" and find nothing left over for themselves. I know my self and my body and my health well enough to know that I am not willing to sacrifice in that area.

I think that we have to be willing to say that I will give "this much" to my career and "this much" to my family and personal life and "this much" to my health and well-being. In other words, like so many areas of our lives (and teaching careers!) there needs to be a comfortable *balance*!

Multiage teacher, California

I always ate breakfast, and protected my lunch break as sacred time to spend with peers and to eat.

Elementary teacher, Colorado

Balance through involvement in school

Sometimes involvement in teaching is a source of joy for teachers, and although they are busy at the job almost all their waking hours, they feel they have chosen this path. School can help teachers get their minds off the stresses in their personal lives. Often they immerse themselves in teaching because they do not have many family demands and often their families are sources of strength.

I have few stresses in my personal life at this time. Perhaps I have very little personal life right now because I choose to spend lots of time planning and learning to be a good teacher. My child is grown and doing well on his own, my parents are relatively healthy and my partner is just as busy with his work as I am with mine. I get lots of warmth, hugs and support from him every day. Having been a single parent for seventeen years, it feels like bliss.

First-grade teacher, Michigan

I don't find that stress in my personal life affects my teaching often. I find that a child's amusing comment can remind me how important my job is and I am usually able to separate my personal life from my classroom. I am sure, however, that there are times that I am a bit on edge with my students because of a personal stress. Hopefully, my students know me well enough to just realize I am having a bad day.

Third-grade teacher, Ohio

Dealing with troublesome teenagers at home, marital stresses—all these had to affect my teaching (especially when they interfered with at-home planning and paper grading), but I found that teaching provided enormous solace—I couldn't worry about my own petty problems when I was managing a class full of kids. The kids' sensitivity and caring often helped a great deal.

High school teacher, California

The demands on my time are the biggest stresses. Needing to be home and at school! Aah! I have started to set limits on my school time, like making every Monday night my running night with friends, every Tuesday night my pottery class. It does stress me to *have* to leave school by a certain time (I like to work methodically until the work is done), but I realize I also need more balance in my life.

First-grade teacher, Oregon

Many teachers report that they attain balance by pursuing hobbies and interests. The next chapter focuses on the ways that they strive for balance through hobbies and interests outside of the demands of school and family.

7

Taking Time for Ourselves

I love to "throw pots" to relieve stress. It is wonderful. I have a friend who is a potter and who gives "therapy sessions," classes. We talk and laugh and make pots!

Kindergarten teacher, Pennsylvania

I believe in the "Spiritual World." I find myself praying from time to time and that always seems to help me stay focused.

Kindergarten teacher, Wyoming

WHEN I taught kindergarten, simple balance scales were part of the standard math equipment in my classroom. The children would load each side with as many blocks as possible until one side toppled over and some of the blocks fell out. Given time, they would start the process over again, striving for balance, which they attained when they became more attentive to the number and kinds of blocks that they used. Our lives sometimes become unbalanced and the blocks in the personal and professional sides of our lives tumble out. With time and choice, we too can regain the balance.

Some of the children began to notice the arrow in the middle of the scale, which was centered when the two dishes of blocks were balanced. Even when the sides weren't precisely even, the arrow didn't move very much, and only when the balance shifted did the arrow fall away from the focal point. Like the arrow of a primary school balance scale, we can stay centered even when our professional or personal lives are weighed down. As long as our arrow is near the center, we can cope with and even benefit from the disequilibrium. In fact, perfect balance might suggest boredom and stagnation, rather than engagement and growth.

As we have observed, trying to balance our personal and professional lives is more than a full-time job, which can leave little or no time for us to develop our own interests and hobbies or to nourish our spiritual life. And yet, taking this time for ourselves in essential in our quest to being centered and balanced.

Developing Our Interests and Hobbies

Teachers reported various pastimes, side interests, and personal projects that help them relieve stress and achieve balance. These hobbies and interests, which they pursue both individually and with others, include exercise, music, crafts and handwork, gardening, reading, travel, church participation, volunteer work, and keeping up with friends.

General responses

Many teachers draw upon a variety of activities beyond the usual demands and obligations of school and family. Being aware of what we personally need to keep ourselves balanced in our lives is an essential first step in relieving stress.

> Any stress in personal life can affect teaching. Teaching is very demanding and requires that we are 100 percent physically and mentally. Of course that is usually not the case. I cope by getting more rest and personal time, talking to friends, praying, listening to music, reading.
>
> *Reading specialist, California*

> Doing something just for me makes me feel like I have accomplished something else besides just schoolwork.
>
> *High school teacher, Minnesota*

> I guess my answer to stress is to have or make plans to do, things I want to do, both school-related and personal/family-related. Hav-

ing something to look forward to outside of school certainly helps. The main ways I relieve school-related stress or cope with burnout is by finding something new that interests me and working on that.

Middle school teacher, Georgia

I am secretary for the local Girl Guide Division. I also belong to the Guide Trefoil League.

Kindergarten teacher, Canada

In searching for a workable balance between personal and professional time, many teachers suggest that it helps to schedule their recreation time by the week. Once the school year begins, they realize that they have to defer some of their hobbies and interests to vacations.

I try to keep *one* weekend day for errands, doing things with family, nonwork stuff; but it isn't always possible. A big help is the fun of looking forward to the next family vacation—we travel a lot, so there is something to anticipate every year. Recently, I have also started to go to a gym two or three times a week.

Teacher educator, California

Part of the balance involves including various kinds of recreation, interests, and hobbies.

I love art, mainly pottery and photography. I have a wheel and a kiln and time spent with clay always helps me balance and reconnect. I also read huge amounts and love to use books to help me reconnect. I love educational books and spiritual books. I am also lucky to run across a great novel sometimes as well.

Preschool teacher, Ohio

I deal with the stresses in my life by talking on a daily basis with a very close group of friends, including my next oldest sister, a professor from my master's program, and several teacher friends. I pray when I remember to. I write in my notebook every day while my kids at school do and I try to keep a sense of humor and perspective about the whole thing. I also belong to several listservs for support and entertainment. I play the piano for my own pleasure. I hold my dogs and get millions of catalogs in the mail. I sew when I am so compelled. I try new laundry products and approaches. I iron my clothes every morning and get up early enough to read (e-mail, books, or magazines) for about ten minutes in peace.

Fifth-grade teacher, South Dakota

I crave time outdoors hiking, swimming, canoeing, and cross-country skiing. I also spend forty-five minutes every morning pray-ing and reading the scriptures and journaling. My family also is a wonderful support to me in terms of balance because they let me know when I am too preoccupied with school. They help me to keep my priorities straight. My wife and I try to walk together every day and that also is a real stress reducer. It is a ministry to my spirit to feel the cool night air on my face and to look up at a full moon or see Orion sparkling in the evening sky.

Fourth-grade teacher, Oregon

I walk, garden, sew, embroider, play the piano, do volunteer work, spend a lot of time at church and in spiritual pursuits at home. I hike, cross-country ski, and swim. I maintain my interest in sci-ence by taking challenging classes and reading scientific litera-ture. I work on a district committee that is doing a lot of good things to bring the requirements of effective science teaching to district administrators and to the school board. This helps a lot with the feeling of powerlessness that sometimes afflicts teachers. I pray a lot.

Kindergarten teacher, Oregon

My interests and hobbies include art, music, drama, reading, and walking. I feel these help me in balancing stress and give me a cre-ative outlet.

First-grade teacher, Ohio

Friends

Teachers are isolated from other adults in most teaching situations, and when they do get together their conversation centers around school-related issues. To counterbalance this, many find that per-sonal relationships with friends are essential to their well-being.

These include other teachers, family members, and friends not involved in teaching.

> Perhaps the best way I relieve my stress is by sharing my reflections online with a trusted friend. I seem to just spill forth the waters of the ocean to her. We talk about everything from classroom practice, current research, books we are reading, family woes, to the ever-present stresses of trying to get everything done. Mostly, she just listens, but from time to time she offers suggestions, or a word, that makes me think about teaching, learning, or my life in a new way. Having her read my thoughts without jumping into what Parker Palmer calls the "quick fix" mode allows me to get out all my feelings, feel safe, and rethink my thoughts. I feel I have grown much from this friendship. It is a treasured relationship, rare and most precious.
>
> *Kindergarten teacher, Indiana*

> I guess most of all, I love my girlfriends. I have frequent "girl dates," where we would meet for lunch or just tea and chatter for hours. I don't think there is anything that brings such contentedness to me as a really great, in-depth conversation.
>
> *Preschool teacher, Ohio*

> Exercise as a stress reducer. I go the Y five mornings a week, before I go to school. In the evenings I often go for walk with my neighbor who is also a teacher. We discuss our work, family, plans, etc.—a great stress reducer. We even walk most of the winter, unless it is too slippery. When it gets really cold, we just have shorter walks.
>
> *Kindergarten teacher, British Columbia*

Solitary hobbies

Unlike many other professions, teachers have very little time to be alone during the school day. They are continually relating to their students who are always present. I found that I liked to get up early so I could have some time by myself, both at home and in my classroom before staff and students filled the building.

> Naturally, I love to garden. (I am a kinder*garden* teacher, after all!)
>
> *Kindergarten teacher, Wyoming*

I enjoy quilting, watching moves, and reading because they all take me away from the pressures of work.

High school teacher, Minnesota

Exercise and travel

Exercise is essential in our quest for balance, but often the busyness of job and family makes it difficult to obtain it on a regular basis. For some teachers, exercise takes the form of a recreational hobby, such as playing tennis or hiking. Others build exercise into their daily routine by walking or working out at a gym.

I must exercise at least four days a week in order to keep balanced. I take the dog running and work out at the club on the cold Minnesota days. This is my quiet time for me, away from work and home.

High school teacher, Minnesota

Hiking is also important—I walk two miles a day and love to hike during spring, summer, and fall.

Language arts teacher, Virginia

Going out and dancing is another way I try to diffuse some of the energy that gets built up in our profession. I have also taken on aerobics as a personal hobby and challenge during these last two years. I say a challenge because I am not athletically inclined. However, I have decided to take better care of myself—to balance head nourishment with body nourishment. I love it! After a hard day's work a good workout really makes a difference and I feel bad when I don't go.

First-grade teacher, Ecuador

I am very athletic . . . I run, play tennis, play basketball, walk, do aerobics, and dance.

Middle school teacher, New York

Getting away. A wonderful ten-day vacation with my husband to Oregon and Washington was a terrific stress reducer for me. I didn't know how much I needed it until I was there.

Resource room teacher, Ohio

Music, crafts, and reading

Teachers also enjoy sedentary hobbies that help them take their minds off the intensity of their jobs and families and give them a varied sense of accomplishment.

> Music—listening to opera, string quartets, baroque, and classical. I play music while I read, prepare dinner, grade papers, and drive in the car. Attending recitals and ballet is something I need. Each year my husband and I subscribe to a series of six to eight recitals at Kennedy Center. I work my entire schedule around these concerts. We make it a day of dinner and music or ballet. Even though we drive for an hour and forty-five minutes, it's totally relaxing. We can talk on the drive and the concert stays with us for it's part of our memories.
>
> *Middle school teacher, Virginia*

> I play the violin with an orchestra. Although I enjoy it, work keeps me busy and I am not finding the time to practice as much as I'd like.
>
> *Elementary teacher, Indiana*

> I could not have gotten through my recent surgery without my cross-stitch, so I must say that I find cross-stitch to be a stress reliever. I usually pick themes like antique Santas or chickens or gardening or kitchen items that I can use in the house. I made stockings for three children and my husband, but have not done mine yet. It requires some thinking because it is counted and uses different colors of thread, but the stitch is very repetitious and can be done with little thought.
>
> *Middle school teacher, Georgia*

> I find I must consciously carve time to read books for myself. I try to keep up with children's books and professional books and find time to write and that's a lot. It's important to just say, "This is for me." And do it.
>
> *Middle school teacher, Virginia*

> I write poetry and memoirs. I draw and I took a watercolor class. In the summer I garden walk. But I forget these things for most of the school year.
>
> *First-grade teacher, Michigan*

Teachers' Suggestions for Taking Care of Ourselves

- Write in my journal.
- Listen to music—classical, cajun, jazz.
- Listen to music tapes in my car—help me to slow down.
- Stay with friends in an inexpensive motel and watch movies all night long.
- Shop.
- Get involved in a project.
- Bowl twice a week.
- Go to exercise class.
- Walk.
- Read friends' recommended novels during the summer.
- Sew and quilt.
- Take bubble baths and listen to relaxing music.
- Watch the sunset.
- Play scrabble.
- Go to church.
- Pray.
- Go out with friends who are not teachers.
- Tell myself that I will only do schoolwork for a specific amount of time, and then stop.
- E-mail a friend.

Nourishing Our Spiritual Life

I was going to quit my church choir because I though I should be planning for my classroom instead of going to Thursday night rehearsals. But I'm not going to. I need to sing in my choir.

Second-grade teacher, New Jersey

Basically I think I'd have to say that teachers have to deal with their own psychological and spiritual issues constantly in order to work with the kids. If you don't have your own stuff in order, you can't possibly get clear with adolescents or younger students.

High school teacher, California

Up to this point we have focused primarily on concrete experiences and everyday actions that teachers take to stay balanced. Behind these activities, however, teachers expressed that they are most successful in finding balance when they feel centered and that this includes nurturing their spiritual life. The variety of ways that they describe how their "calling, vocation, and/or life purpose" helps them stay centered are unique, personal, and profound, and show the depth, seriousness, and openness with which they enter the classroom each day. And yet, as individual and specific as their comments are, universal themes resonate throughout their words. For some, this encompasses a general belief in a higher cause, while for others it involves a specific religious tradition or faith community. Many teachers have an articulated specific mission statement or life purpose that guides their work

Asking the big questions

In their quest to make the world a better place to live, teachers are continually asking themselves the big questions about life, and are listening and learning from others. They are willing to live on what Martin Buber (1996) calls "the narrow ridge," a place beyond the objective and the subjective, beyond individualism and collectivism, where they can listen openly and learn from others and perhaps come to new understandings.

> I think we all should be asking questions—questions about how humans really ought to live. The question isn't, "Why isn't this a perfect world?" It is, "How can I help make this a better world for everyone?" In doing that, we need to discuss our needs, our desires, our dreams, and our stress loads. Maybe, in the midst of the talking, someone with more experience will give a right answer to someone needing it, or maybe we will make a change for the better.
>
> *Third-grade teacher, New York*

Through the work of Piaget, teachers know that disequlibrium invites new learning. This tension or imbalance in their thinking propels them to consider different ways of responding to their current teaching situation and personal circumstances. Tension is a necessary part of being human. It's what makes us grow and "mature," if you will. Tension is that piece that's necessary for learning to take place. I guess the tension becomes "bad" when we allow ourselves to get "distracted" from our goals and lose sight of our purposes; we start worrying about the details or the petty conversations going on around us. I think when I stop looking at my kids and their needs, I know I've been distracted. I always have to keep my students in my mind's eye.

First-grade teacher, Ecuador

Being truthful

The Sanskrit word for virtue is *sila*, and one of its meanings includes being straightforward and honest both with one's self and with others (Surya Das 1997, 137). The clearer we are about our higher purpose, the more truthful we can be both to ourselves and others. Teachers want to express their opinions and be honest about what is important to them, but sometimes their concern of repercussions stops them from speaking out. Then they close their doors and remain silent. Regardless, stress can build up both from speaking out and from remaining silent.

I have found that being direct with people and promptly apologizing for incorrect behavior helps me with a lot of my stress. But when that's not possible, I pray, knit, get more sleep, cuddle with my cats and my husband, and talk to those who might know how to help me. Stress comes from wanting to do or say something but not being able to because we fearing repercussions. We feel caged in. Teachers face these situations in some form or other, and we all have to deal with them.

High school teacher, Ohio

I have been experiencing another stress lately that comes off and on. It is the stress of being an atheist in a society that seems to consider my beliefs tantamount to devil worship. I believe very strongly that we are all brothers and sisters, responsible to and for each other. When attending school board meetings and some school functions I worry about reactions from people around me when I do not bow my head during the opening prayer or say "amen." Sometimes I am so worried that I just look at the floor so people assume I am part of the prayer. But it is stressful for me to do that as well because I feel like a hypocrite. I would like people to know that I am a good person, a caring person, a hardworking person and that I do not have to believe in a deity or organized religion to be that kind of person.

Kindergarten teacher, Michigan

Spiritual orientations

Again and again teachers stated that a spiritual orientation or specific religious tradition was essential to their success in balancing their personal and professional lives and staying centered.

Absolutely! My faith helps me remember why I do what I do, and for whom I do it. Lately I have had tremendous stress from district-level politics and the state-level interference, and it would take me down completely, but I remind myself that I am serving a higher person. It literally keeps me from quitting.

Curriculum specialist, California

Music functions as a spiritual orientation to me.

High school English teacher, California

My training in acting is really my spiritual training—and helps tremendously in dealing with stress.

Sixth-grade teacher, Ohio

When I am horribly stressed, which is usually not school-related, I pray. I pray a lot.

Kindergarten teacher, California

A belief in God's controlling power and some good books on positive thinking help.

High school teacher, Georgia

As for my faith, it is very personal and I have to watch who I speak to because some people are offended and feel I am preaching. There is a guidance in my life that has my best interest in mind. I may not always know why something happened, good or bad, but there is a reason for it. It is a feeling that permeates my entire existence. I don't feel I need to follow certain rituals, just lead a good life and do the best I can. The label of the religion doesn't really matter to me. I don't feel my god has to be your god.

Kindergarten teacher, Pennsylvania

Reading and praying help keep a balance. It seems like my mind is always working. If I'm not thinking about something to do with my family, I'm thinking about how to present lessons so that I can reach the most kids. Both reading and praying help my mind "take a vacation." I can then return to problems in my mind with a fresh look.

Third-grade teacher, Arizona

Specific religious traditions

Many teachers are centered through specific faith traditions:

I am a Baha'i and therefore I study and learn about all beliefs, honoring them all. I love to listen and learn as others share their beliefs. I love to ask questions to learn, but feel strongly never to question or debate someone's spiritual beliefs. The key is to refrain from judgment and look for the teaching in each situation. I think that this belief helps me not to get defensive and to stay centered so I can learn from it and move forward.

Preschool teacher, Ohio

The other area of interest for me began with multicultural education while I was a graduate student. It, however, has emerged as a focus in race unity, mostly through work that I do as a Baha'i. We Baha'is are of all nations and all ethnicities, all races and all former religions. . . . The faith moves me to reach for greater heights.

Elementary teacher, Vermont

I am currently studying Buddhism. It is a way of life much more than a religion. The teachings have helped me to live life each moment. I practice meditation, which helps me to know myself better, and to see things in a new light. It has deepened my understanding of the world and of my teaching practice.

Preschool teacher, Arizona

My Christian faith roots me well. Remembering to live my life to glorify the lord and not myself helps me to remember the burden is easy and the yolk is light.

First-grade teacher, California

I attend my family church that I grew up in and feel a sense of community, love, and welcomeness. It helps to make me feel whole.

Middle school teacher, Minnesota

I am not religious in terms of dogma or regular participation in rituals, but have a background attitude that is calming: I am a Quaker by choice.

Teacher educator, California

I believe my faith in God, my church, and prayers help me deal daily with stress. I go to church regularly, and God does guide me in whatever I do. I pray for help and guidance often.

Kindergarten teacher, California

I am very involved in church. My husband and I are the youth pastors there. Christ plays a huge role in my life. He is so important to me and to my family.

Middle school teacher, New York

Yes. My husband pastors a Pentecostal church. Prayer and attending church are a great help in dealing with stress.

Third-grade teacher, Arizona

We are very active in our synagogue and have a very supportive group of friends who are like family.

Kindergarten teacher, New Hampshire

My teaching job, needless to say, requires a tremendous amount of time and energy. It is, in many ways, more than a full-time endeavor. Many of my relatives and friends cannot understand how, in addition to my teaching, I am also a cantor who works every Friday night. I often ask myself how I do it, because it requires a second wind that is not always available. I do it because it restores my spirit, my soul. I always leave services on Friday evenings feeling more whole, more in touch with the person who resides deep within the core of my existence.

Third-grade teacher, New York

Religious callings

Many teachers wrote that their spiritual tradition has called them to teaching, and that this calling guides their daily work in the classroom. These callings involve theological, psychological, and sociological questions. Theologically, we ask what place God (the Divine, or the Power of a higher being) plays in our teaching vocation. Psychologically, our childhood experiences affect how and why we want to help those who are in the midst of childhood. Sociologically, our particular culture, ethnicity, and social status affect what we want and whom and where we teach.

Yes, my Christian faith is the power behind my work with children and the source of my inspiration and success. I believe that my ability to teach and to really reach children is a gift from God and that my teaching is my ministry and life's work. This has been a source of inspiration and strength that has kept me alive and vital as a teacher. I love teaching more than I did when I first went into it and I believe that is confirmation of the fact that it is a gift from God.

Science specialist, Oregon

A friend asked me why I left a good paying job to spend five years in college and make less while working in what he considered deplorable conditions of my teaching situation. My reason . . . because I need to make a difference! I know that *God* put me on this planet to touch the lives of children. When I'm stressed, I think about what my life would be like if I had not become a teacher. I'd never know the joy of teaching a child to read or speak English. Why do I put up with all of the "special circumstances" I have to deal with? Because I'm here to touch children and I'm thankful that I actually know why *God* put me on this planet.

Literacy specialist, California

I believe my teaching is a vocational call. (I tried to ignore it as long as I could.) I believe that God has commissioned me to this vocation and will give me the strength and spirit I need to carry on.

Elementary teacher, California

Role Models

In response to the question "Are there persons in your life who have served as role models?" teachers mentioned family members and friends, and teachers and administrators both past and present. Some wrote about one special person, while others listed several important mentors in their lives.

A wonderful principal, many capable teachers with whom I've been privileged to work. There have been many others in non-teaching roles who inspire me as well, such as my minister and others who make love their aim

Multiage teacher, California

Family members

I believe we are all here to teach each other, and with this awareness we experience growth. My husband is my role model on how to conduct myself as a member of the human race. He helps me to stay centered and look objectively at people and all situations with a kind, loving, and accepting heart. My children help me always to look at life through the eyes of a learner with wonder and excitement (they also play a pretty good mirror when I need to look at something for myself). I have many friends and colleagues who inspire me to be a better learner, professional, artist, woman, mother, naturalist, child, parent, person, etc.

Early childhood teacher, Ohio

First and foremost is my mother. She worked very hard in her life for her family. She taught me to forgive, to be patient, and to love life. She is a very wonderful person.

Middle school teacher, Minnesota

My dad—he was very family-oriented and a very caring, warm person.

Primary teacher, New Hampshire

My grandfather was an excellent teacher and that is why I became a teacher educator.

Mathematics teacher, Minnesota

My parents, my sister, my husband, my in-laws, and Jesus Christ are my role models.

English teacher, New York

My grandmother, cousin, and some teaching friends.

Kindergarten teacher, Canada

My husband teaches, too, but always manages to find time for himself! I resent that at times. But it's always my choice how I choose to spend my time, and I know that.

First-grade teacher, Oregon

My husband, who reaches his goals and goes after his dreams. He also taught me how to truly appreciate others. My sister, a dedicated mother, my grandfather, a quiet man, and my dad for teaching me that you need to understand the rules and why you follow them. This means questioning "authority." Or perhaps it was more like teaching me, "You need to choose who you put yourself under." My great aunt, an ex-nun with her doctorate in physics who spends her retirement caring for the (other) elderly in her community and volunteers as a reading teacher at the local elementary school. (She taught for years with as many as sixty in an elementary class and also taught methods courses while still in her order.)

First-grade teacher, California

Mainly my husband, who takes life at a much slower pace. He's taught me to slow down and enjoy each moment.

Middle school teacher, Virginia

Teachers

Some teachers wrote about teachers that they had when they were in school who were role models and who were catalysts for choosing teaching as a career.

> My third-grade teacher. I would never want to be like her but I enjoyed her class more than any other I can remember. She was a passionate teacher! Some of my teachers and coaches. They taught me that hard work always pays off.
>
> *Middle school teacher, Minnesota*

> Yes! My acting teacher, who taught me in middle school and high school, and still teaches me to this day, is a true inspiration. I model my teaching after hers. She refuses to answer questions— she only asks them. Being her student is frustrating and wonderful; you must think for yourself and invent solutions to problems. Working with her stretched my mind to its limits and beyond!
>
> *Elementary teacher, Virginia*

Current and past colleagues

> The people in my life who are role models would be my friends who are teachers. They understand the problems without explanation, they listen and offer sound advice. I hope I do the same for them.
>
> *Kindergarten teacher, Pennsylvania*

> My most important role model was my first teaching partner, who taught me about using humor to deal with stress, that love is more important than content, and that digging ditches might seem a better alternative than teaching on field trip day. I have been privileged to know and teach with many wonderful teachers through the years and I hope that I carry a little piece of what is best about each one of them with me every time I go to school.
>
> *Fifth-grade teacher, South Dakota*

> I am always open to people who have new or different ideas and new ways of thinking about other ideas, so I tend to seek out

people I feel I can learn something from. I have always had teacher friends that I have tried to get inside of their brains to see what I could learn. My current role model is a teacher of teachers. Knowing her has been a mind-expanding experience. I am still learning from her.

Second-grade teacher, Indiana

My third-grade and high school English teachers have served as role models in my life. Their dedication and commitment to teaching children has always been with me.

Teacher educator, California

I would say a sixth-grade teacher I had served as a role model for me. She encouraged me as a new student in the school and put a stop to the antics of some bullies. She also invited my younger brother to her farm where she showed him various tasks. The caring and concern she showed was wonderful. Another role model for me was a teacher I had when I was in high school. I had just transferred from California to Montana and had thus started the year late. In California school starts after Labor Day, but in Montana it started in August. I signed up for a math class and my test grades at first were awful. The teacher just said, "Oh, I know you know how to do this." His confidence in me soon had me turning in papers that received As. I have tried to carry that over to my children and my students. What I believe they can do, they will do. Whatever their potential is, if I believe in them, they will be given the key to reach for the stars.

Third-grade teacher, Arizona

One of my mentors was a college professor who taught me to know my work and to use what I know to make decisions. She was never as interested in how I was conducting a lesson as much as why I was doing it the way that I was. She taught me to really think through my teaching and to make sure that my teaching matched my philosophy. Because she taught me to always know why I do what I do, my stress in the classroom is low because I feel confident that I am doing the right thing for kids.

Preschool teacher, Ohio

I've had many mentors over the years but the greatest influence has been from colleagues.

First-grade teacher, Texas

Administrators

Teachers wrote about administrators, past and present, who are role models to them. These administrators supported them in both their personal and professional lives and gave them confidence when they most needed it. They also model professionalism, hard work, and personal commitment.

My best role model in education was my first principal. Whether it was because I was so impressionable, I don't know. He taught me how to balance my life. He taught me how to teach. He validated a young teacher. I needed that. I will never forget my experience with him.

Kindergarten teacher, California

Yes, there are persons in my life who have served as role models. Numerous people have crossed paths with me of which I am very grateful. Probably the most important person in my professional life is my former assistant principal. We still e-mail each other about once a month. She is an incredible leader and teacher.

Elementary teacher, Wyoming

I also look up to a few administrators whom I have worked for because they are very good at balancing public relations, talking with students, parents, and the public, doing scheduling, preparing the budget, and simply going with the flow of whatever the day brings them. That is what administration is all about.

Kindergarten teacher, Oregon

My high school principal, who is now my superintendent. He believed in me when I didn't believe in myself. My whole language methods instructor. I respect her for standing her ground in California today.

First-grade teacher, California

Finally, some teachers were beginning to realize that they were becoming role models for their students.

> I feel joy when former students remember something good that happened when I was their teacher and shares that memory with me.
>
> *Fifth-grade teacher, South Dakota*

We have seen that taking time for ourselves is an essential component in our quest to be centered and obtain balance in our lives. The better we understand ourselves and understand our particular life situation, the better able we are to attain a state of centering and balance. Part Two explores some of the strategies that I have personally found useful in this search and that I have shared with teachers.

8

Creating a Personal Inventory

IN PART One we heard classroom teachers describe their experiences inside and outside the classroom and explain how they strive to balance their personal and professional lives and stay centered. In some respects, they make it seem somewhat easy, but behind the solutions are struggles and hard work.

Although we can apply some of their suggestions to our own lives, we need to create our own answers to some of the essential questions about our well-being. For example, How can I create a balance between my professional and personal life that supports my particular situation and personality? How can I provide time for family, friends, and personal interests? How can I stay centered in the midst of stress and increasing demands in my life? How can I take care of myself? Part Two provides some strategies for solutions to these questions.

I have found that the better I understand myself, the better I am able to deal with stress and stay centered. In workshops with teachers, I have shared some of the strategies that I have used to help find balance and centering in my own life. These involve personal reflections, learning from childhood memories, creating nuggets of truth, exploring spirituality, taking positive action, writing mission statements, and taking time for ourselves. These strategies are described in the following chapters and are accompanied by optional reflection sections. You might want to take extra time and write your reflections in a personal journal.

One way actively to start working toward balance in our professional and personal lives is to take stock of our current situation. In this chapter you are asked to focus on different aspects of your life, such as personal obligations, your professional situation, personal interests and dreams, and stress points that you encounter both in school and out of school, and to consider how you can respond positively to the stresses and worries that occur. In parts one and two, take stock of your current personal and professional circumstances. In part three, record some of your interests and dreams and consider ways to pursue and fulfill them. In part four, examine the different areas in your life that bring on stress and consider strategies to help alleviate those stresses. Again, the four parts are:

1. my personal situation
2. my professional situation
3. my interests and dreams
4. understanding and managing my stress points: inside school and outside of school

In responding to the various reflections, please keep the following in mind—there are no right or wrong answers. Whatever you write will support you in creating balance and in being centered. Treat yourself to an hour alone to fill out the inventory. Settle into a comfortable chair, provide yourself with a favorite snack, turn on your favorite music. Be good to yourself as you allow yourself to be centered.

1. Personal Situation

The first reflection is designed to help you look closely at the personal obligations in your life. Under each category list all your obligations and be descriptive and specific in naming them. For example, under family situation: *be a mom to my three children; take my father to the doctor every week*, under civic obligations: *member of religious education committee at church; work at the town food pantry once a month*. Don't limit yourself to the lines provided; use an additional piece of paper. Write any personal comments in your separate journal.

Family Situation (spouse, partner, children, parents)

———————

———————

———————

———————

———————

Civic Obligations (church, temple, town/city committees)

———————

———————

———————

———————

———————

Other Obligations

———————

———————

———————

———————

2. Professional Situation

This reflection asks you to examine your professional situation. Check all the categories that apply to you and put an asterisk before those that currently have a high impact on your life. For example, if you are a first-year teacher you may find that you are spending every weekend on school-related activities and have no time for recreation with friends or family; you may teach in an urban school that must be locked an hour after school closes, limiting the time to work in your classroom; or you may have two sessions of kindergarten with more than thirty children in each session. Next, check all your professional commitments, such as membership on the science committee, or liaison with the parent-teacher organization. Finally, write down future teaching aspirations and goals, which might include writing an article, giving a workshop, and getting involved with a state or national teaching organization.

Teaching Experience

_____ first-year teacher

_____ two to seven years

_____ seven to ten years

_____ ten to twenty-five years

_____ more than twenty-five years

_____ thinking of retiring

Teaching Location

_____ rural

_____ suburban

_____ urban

_____ other

Teaching Position

_____ primary

_____ upper elementary

_____ middle school

_____ high school

_____ classroom teacher

_____ specialist

_____ administrator

_____ teacher educator

_____ other

Professional Obligations

_____ curriculum committees

_____ grade level meetings

_____ team meetings about specific children

_____ study groups

_____ other

_____

_____

_____

Professional Aspirations and Goals (positions, leadership roles, education, publication)

_____

_____

_____

_____

3. Interests and Dreams

Now think about those interests and dreams that you would like to develop but never feel you have time to pursue. These are those aspects of your life that you know make you a better teacher, but often get shortchanged.

Complete the statements following each category (listed in alphabetical order). First, record activities that you are currently doing and want to continue. For example, *Currently I take a twenty-minute walk every day* or *Currently I spend Saturday mornings taking a painting course.* Next, list what you would like to do but aren't presently accomplishing. These activities may be in the realm of possibility for you, such as, *I would like to read for pleasure for half an hour each day,* or *I would like to help in a soup kitchen once a month,* or they may seem like pure fantasy, such as wanting to climb Mount McKinley. Finally, list any activities that you would like to do less, such as, *I would like to spend less time going to the grocery store.*

_____ **Community service**

Currently I _____.

I would like to _____.

I would like to do less _____.

_____ **Entertainment**

Currently I _____.

I would like to _____.

I would like to do less _____.

_____ **Exercise**

Currently I _____.

I would like to _____.

I would like to do less _____.

_____ **Family fun**

Currently I _____.

I would like to _____.

I would like to do less _____.

_____ **Friendships**

Currently I _____.

I would like to _____.

I would like to do less _____.

_____ **Hobbies**

Currently I _____.

I would like to _____.

I would like to do less _____.

_____ **Reading**

Currently I _____.

I would like to _____.

I would like to do less _____.

_____ **Relaxation**

Currently I _____.

I would like to _____.

I would like to do less _____.

_____ **Solitude**

Currently I _____.

I would like to _____.

I would like to do less _____.

_____ **Teaching**

Currently I _____.

I would like to _____.

I would like to do less _____.

_____ **Writing**

Currently I _____.

I would like to _____.

I would like to do less _____.

After you have completed the inventory, go back and put a check before one or two new activities that you could begin to include immediately in your life, *and begin today.* This may mean making a call about the dance class you want to join, taking a bubble bath after the children have gone to bed, or planning a family mystery trip for the weekend. Second, put a star before one of the activities that seems impractical or fanciful, and take a small step toward making it a reality. For example, if you want to climb Mount McKinley, get some hiking boots and plan a hike for the weekend or your next vacation. Finally, check an activity you would like to decrease or eliminate, and begin to do less of it.

4. Understanding and Managing Stress Points

In order to fulfill your professional and personal obligations and pursue your interests and dreams, it is important to understand the areas of stress in your life and develop strategies to relieve them.

In this reflection, first, rank in order from 1 to 8 the areas of stress for you both inside and outside of school, with 8 being the most stressful and 1 being the least stressful. Next, respond to the questions under each category.

In school

_____ **Time management**

I get stressed when _____.

It helps when _____.

I want to try _____.

_____ **Getting everything done**

I get stressed when _____.

It helps when _____.

I want to try _____.

_____ **Curriculum responsibilities**

I get stressed when _____.

It helps when _____.

I want to try _____.

_____ **Teaching each child**

I get stressed when _____.

It helps when _____.

I want to try _____.

_____ **Behavior issues**

I get stressed when _____.

It helps when _____.

I want to try _____.

_____ **Standardized tests**

I get stressed when _____.

It helps when _____.

I want to try _____.

_____ **School atmosphere**

I get stressed when _____.

It helps when _____.

I want to try _____.

_____ **School administration mandates**

I get stressed when _____.

It helps when _____.

I want to try _____.

Now go back and pick one area to work on immediately. You may decide to begin with your most stressful area, or you may feel you will be most successful starting with a less stressful area.

Repeat the same exercises for managing stress out of school.

Out of school

_____ Time management

I get stressed when _____.

It helps when _____.

I want to try _____.

_____ Spending time with family

I get stressed when _____.

It helps when _____.

I want to try _____.

_____ Juggling family schedules

I get stressed when _____.

It helps when _____.

I want to try _____.

_____ Providing meals for the family

I get stressed when _____.

It helps when _____.

I want to try _____.

_____ Keeping the house in order

I get stressed when _____.

It helps when _____.

I want to try _____.

_____ Lacking time for yourself

I get stressed when _____.

It helps when _____.

I want to try _____.

_____ Specific family obligations

I get stressed when _____.

It helps when _____.

I want to try _____.

_____ Civic obligations

I get stressed when _____.

It helps when _____.

I want to try _____.

I hope that the process of filling out this inventory has helped you to assess and reflect upon your personal and professional situation, encouraged you to pursue your interests and dreams, and to take concrete steps toward understanding and managing the stress in your life. You may want to refer to it as you read the next chapters.

9

Learning from Childhood Memories

THE MORE we understand ourselves, the more centered we become. Childhood memories help us discern the present and look to the future. The events and accompanying feelings that we remember from childhood provide powerful mirrors of who we are as unique human beings. They show us our interests, how we go about a task, how we respond to adversity, and offer us the possibility of reaching our unfulfilled dreams. Memories help us form our goals and follow our rules for staying centered.

In this chapter we explore some of our childhood memories. Since this is a centering book for teachers, we will concentrate on two childhood areas that directly correspond to our job as educators: memories of imaginative play and memories of reading and writing both at school and at home, and explore how our childhood memories guide our lives today. Limiting our focus in no way diminishes the importance of other family memories, but they are beyond the scope of this book. You may, however, want to spend time specifically reflecting on them.

Memories of Childhood Play

I pay a great deal of attention to memories of my childhood play because I continually notice parallels to my personal and professional adult life. Many of my present values were formed through my childhood play. What was important back then is important now. In preparation for this book I wrote down these memories and discovered that the two that kept coming to mind were connected to my solitary world and my world with friends, both necessary for my continued search to stay centered:

- climbing the dogwood tree in the front yard: my solitary world
- playing teddy bears with my friend: my world with friends

Childhood Memories

Write down the childhood memories that come quickly to your mind. Use active verbs and clear visual images.

After I came up with my most vivid memories, I wrote about them, allowing the images, lessons, and concepts to flow. I noticed that I had a very distinct picture of each memory, and that if I closed my eyes and let my imagination meander, I could conjure up more images and almost feel that I was back there in the moment. I was amazed at how easy it was to make connections between past experiences, the essential elements in my present life, and my dreams and goals for the future. Finally, I realized that these powerful memories had direct implications for classroom teaching, where children are imagining and creating memories.

Climbing the dogwood tree in the front yard: My solitary world

The dogwood tree in the front yard of my childhood house was mine. No one ever said as much, but my parents and I had that unspoken understanding. The tree offered several constellations of branches that became rooms for my play: a kitchen where I ate crackers, cookies, and candy that I brought from the house; and a living room, which was my thinking room. I spent hours by myself in that tree, creating an imaginary world that often seemed more real than my everyday existence. Although my family often knew I was there, they never asked what I was doing. I never told them that I was discovering unique secrets as I sat in the crook of my favorite branches. I never told them how peaceful I felt as I disappeared amongst the leaves. One day I let a friend play in the tree with me, but I couldn't wait for her to leave. I was afraid she'd discover the secrets held in the tree.

I don't live in that house any more and the tree has been cut down, but from time to time I still imagine myself hidden among its blossoms, where as a child I found time to think, exercise my imagination, fantasize, make important decisions, and time to write and time to center. As an adult I still need periods of solitude for this same kind of thinking, and if I don't get enough alone time each day, I find it difficult to remain centered, especially in times of stress.

Usually I have my alone time in the early morning. I get up, plug in the coffee, feed the dog and cat, and settle into a favorite chair in our sunroom to read, write, and think. I try to spend an hour at this solitude, reading spiritual texts, writing in my journal, and praying and practicing meditation. This is the time when I try to understand any worries I had during the night, anticipate stressful upcoming moments, and plan ways to stay centered throughout the day. (In Chapter 11 we will explore ways to plan some alone time for yourself.)

I spent many wonderful hours of childhood play in solitude, fashioning safe spaces where I could think and create a world that gave meaning to my life—building a fort in a run-down shack in the woods, turning my closet into a secret playroom, setting up an office in the cellar, and making a secret room under a card table at my grandmother's apartment in Brooklyn.

I often wonder about the children we teach. Do they have a favorite tree to climb, or a private spot where they can discover their secrets? Many children don't have the opportunity to be alone or quiet at home. There is no time or place for them to create their imaginary domains. There are no trees, closets, or card tables. For these children especially, we must provide spaces for them to climb into their secret worlds—a big box with a cut out window, an area under a table with pillows, or an overstuffed chair or couch; and we must provide time for them to discover their secrets—when they settle in the morning, during quiet reading and writing, or an extended project or workshop period.

Playing teddy bears: My world with friends

For two years my friend Terry and I lived in our own created world of Oz. Terry was the Tin Woodsman, I was the Scarecrow, and our bikes were scaliwagons. We read all the Oz books and spent every weekend making clothes and furniture for our teddy bears, who were an integral part of our imaginary Oz realm.

No one knew the details of our play or that it consumed such a large portion of our lives. I remember the day Terry brought one of her teddy bears to school. He sat in a chair in the back of the room. What a story that bear could have told! A story of friendship, of creativity, of imagination, of reading and rereading texts. But no one knew, and that was fine with us. In fact, if grown-ups had paid attention, our play would have ended. Children's play needs to be private.

Memories from Imaginative Play

Describe a few pivotal childhood memories from your imaginative play. Start with a freewrite. Get your ideas down quickly. What is the significance of these memories on your life today? How do they affect your teaching? Later, return to the piece and edit for clarity.

Today my adult friends are extremely important to me and I devote a great deal of time keeping in contact with them. We all have a unique history together, some "ancient" and others more contemporary. For example, I've known Debby, to whom I dedicated *Thinking and Learning Together*, since we were two. We were childhood playmates and we still meet for lunch three or four times a year. College friends share memories of blossoming into adulthood. The friends with whom I shared parenting continue to be important because they have an experience of my children's history from birth to adulthood. We help each other appreciate our children *and* let them go. Mildred, who died a few years ago at age 94, was a long-time friend from church. She was writing her memoirs and we'd get together to talk about writing. I've made teacher friends around the country, and I chat with many of them on the phone, over e-mail, and at conferences. My family has always been my friends.

Today I wonder how we can give our students opportunities to learn about friendships. What can we do to foster friendships that can last a lifetime? Many teachers give children time to socialize when they come in the morning. Children develop friendships when they work together on inquiry projects in social studies or science and when the read and write together. They learn the give-and-take of getting along together at recess.

Role Models

List the important people in each of the major stages in your life. How have they been role models to you?

Memories of Reading and Writing

Our memories of school have direct bearing on our professional and personal lives. What do we remember about learning to read and write? Where did we learn to read and write? What experiences stand out in our minds throughout the grades? Do the positive experiences help us stay centered? Do the negative experiences add to the stress in our present lives? How can we learn from both kinds of experiences?

Memories of Learning to Read and Write

The idea for this reflection comes from Carolyn Burke at Indiana University, who asks her graduate students to write about their memories of learning to read and write. Be sure to include memories from both inside and outside the classroom. How do these experiences affect your teaching?

Learning at school

I don't remember very much about learning to read in school. I know we had reading groups but I don't remember which group I was in. In first grade, when our group was called we brought our chairs to the front of the room to form a circle and took turns round robin reading. The stories were about white middle-class families and middle-class animal families. Sometimes we went over our workbooks. I have a more vivid memory of getting the chairs in a circle and the importance of following along so we'd know when our turn came than of what we read or discussed. In third grade, everyone wanted Miss Mary for a teacher because she read "real books" to her class. The magic of these books was that they were her *own* books, brought from faraway Canada, books that she loved. There was something wonderfully mysterious about a teacher owning her own books. This is the most specific memory I have of teachers reading aloud, although I know that others did.

Writing in my elementary years consisted of handwriting and copying sentences from lessons in graded English books. Each lesson focused on a specific grammatical or writing convention. For example, in second grade we copied ten sentences (in our best handwriting, of course) and added the correct ending punctuation, a period, question mark, or exclamation point. It isn't until sixth grade that I remember writing assignments that focused on content. Miss Eddy assigned a weekly essay, and at the beginning of the year she posted the list of topics for the year. The only one I remember was to write about a flower, but I have no recollection of what I wrote. When one class member started handing in the assignments for the entire year, Miss Eddy put a stop to it, suggesting that we would learn new things during the year and that we should write each essay the week before it was due. I think she was trying to help us organize our time by posting the topics but I don't remember any help in writing. She corrected each essay but never conferred with us about them.

My high school English teacher taught me to value my own literacy and listen to my own voice. This was in the fifties, before reading workshop, writing process, and portfolio assessment had been explored. Although we studied some texts in class, our main assignment was to write and read widely, and throughout the year hand in pieces of writing and book reflections for his comments in preparation for creating a journal of personal writing and reading at the end of the year. Mr. Smith sent two important messages that have continued to give me confidence in my adult life: meaning is at the center of writing, and authentic reading and writing stems from one's interests. Thus, although he would "red pencil" our papers, he primarily commented on the ideas and stories in our writing, and on what we found valuable in our reading. Secondly, he gave free choice of writing topics and the books we read. He gave me the confidence to write about my teaching experiences.

Since I was a student in school, teachers have learned a great deal about how people learn to read and write. Educators have spent time in classrooms, observing, interacting, and talking with students about their reading and writing. We know how to help young readers and writers learn the skills and conventions necessary to create a coherent piece of meaningful writing. We also know how important it is to give our students the confidence that they are writers and have important ideas to share. This begins in the early years of schooling, in kindergarten, if not earlier, when children write and draw daily as part of the fabric of their lives in school. Early on they understand that they are valued as human beings with important ideas to explore, read and write about, and share. They don't need to wait or hope for a Mr. Smith in high school.

Every once in a while I meet the parent of a former kindergarten student of mine who tells me that their child, now in high school, loves to write, and that they remember all the writing we did in kindergarten. In that kindergarten writing, which focused primarily on their drawings, they were learning to express and value their five-year-old ideas, interests, and passions, be they dinosaurs, flowers, hockey, horses, or space ships. It warmed my heart recently to read a letter to the editor in our local newspaper about peer mediation written by a former student, now in middle school. I think about the focus on testing now, and hope that teachers can hold onto these values, which are essential but untestable.

Learning at home

At home the purposes for reading and writing were were always meaning centered. I remember a bedtime story every night unless my parents went out. My mom read to me, but my most powerful memories are of my father making up stories about the Thornton Burgess animals and telling them to me as I fell asleep. We had lots of books in the house and were often given them as gifts. Books were an integral part of my play. I read them to my stuffed animals and took them with me as I set up play areas both inside and outside. I constantly referred to information books for science experiments, magic tricks, maps, and specific data and facts. The Oz books served many purposes, were guide books, references, and enjoyable stories that tweaked my imagination and acted as catalysts for my creative play.

My parents were less involved with my writing, except for insisting that I write thank-you letters from time to time, but they supplied me with paper, pencils, crayons, and paints. My writing was part of my play, always meaningful and always self-initiated. I wrote lists, secret messages, notes, schedules, programs, and stories. Sometimes I was the writer and other times I was the "scribe" for my stuffed animals and imaginary play characters.

Memories Guiding the Present

These memories remain strong in my life today, and the truths they revealed then still guide me today. They remind me of what I value and give me the fortitude to pursue my own interests, inclinations, and talents, and to stay away from pursuits for which I have little interest, inclination, or talent. These past memories are food for my adult life, my adult play.

My childhood play in the dogwood tree reminds me that I need a great deal of time by myself to let my imagination create and explore. During this alone time I worked through many of my teaching structures as well as ways to share them with teachers in workshops, publications, and now over the Internet. My teddy bear play with my friend Terry was practice for my years with young children as a classroom teacher.

During this alone time I have spent time thinking about theological questions of life: Why are we here? Why do good things happen to bad people? How is dying part of living? What about God? Early in my adult life I started spending time each morning reading and thinking about these questions, and the practice has never stopped. Presently I am studying for a master's of divinity as part of this quest and as training to help teachers in their spiritual journey. The dialectic of solitude and socializing is finding unity in this present work.

The positive reading and writing experiences from high school have helped me pursue my writing career, from personal journal writing to professional publication. Mr. Smith's confidence in the value of ideas and meaning in writing gave me the support to "have a go" and take the risk to hand in a proposal to Heinemann back in 1989.

My parents valued me as an individual and gave me the time to purse my own interest in my particular way. I'm willing to give things a try and to enjoy the journey on the way, regardless of the outcome. Presently I'm writing a children's book about Florence Italy in the fifteenth century and the building of the Duomo. It may never get published, but the project creates a focus for reading and study, as well as travel. And yet, maybe it will. Regardless, I love the journey.

Memories Guiding the Present

How do your past memories guide what you do today? What parallels can you draw between your interests as a child and your interests as an adult?

10

Exploring Truths and Spirituality

Creating Nuggets of Truth

VIRGINIA WOOLF, in the introduction to *A Room of One's Own*, says that she understands that the duty of a lecturer is to offer "a nugget of pure truth to wrap up between the pages of your notebooks and keep on the mantel-piece for ever." In 1963, while studying for my master's in teaching at Wheelock College in Boston, I received a nugget of truth that I wrote in my journal: "We must honor and trust ourselves just as we do the other adults and children in our lives." Rather than placing that nugget on a shelf, I have carried it with me into my personal and professional life and have tried to act upon it to help myself stay centered. Sometimes I have been successful and sometimes I have failed. Nevertheless, the truth is always there for me: "Treat *all* people with respect and dignity." When I keep that nugget at the center of what I do, I create opportunities for truth for myself and the people around me.

I find that when things are going well, I seem to follow these nuggets naturally. Life has an easy flow about it and I view worries as opportunities for growth. In fact, if I were always centered, I wouldn't need to be conscious of these nuggets. However, when worries arise I must be mindful of those nuggets so I can call on them to turn negative situations into positive opportunities. Thinking of them when there is joy is one way to do this. Practicing them when there is stress helps me stay centered in potentially tough situations.

In this chapter I discuss some of the nuggets that support me in my quest to stay centered and to balance my professional and personal life, and ask you to examine the nuggets of truth that bring you joy and peace and that help you deal positively with worry and stress.

My Nuggets of Truth

- Before you read my nuggets, write down your own. There are no right or wrong answers, and no correct number, but try to come up with at least five. Whatever you write will support you in being centered. However, I suggest that you write them in a positive voice. For example, my second nugget is, *Spend time with positive people*, rather than, *Don't spend time with negative people*.
- After you've had your first go at writing your nuggets, give yourself a break: take a walk, laugh with friends, get a good night's sleep, and return to the list tomorrow. When you feel your list is complete, read on, but feel free to continually add to and edit it. Cross out, but don't erase. Your initial responses hold the important truths of the moment and you will want to look back from time to time to observe your process. You may want to use different colored pens to differentiate first drafts from subsequent writings. If you're writing in a separate journal, rewrite the list as you gain new insights. Be sure to date each one.

Take time for myself, my family, and my friends

The theme of this book is that to stay centered and respond proactively to worry and stress both inside and outside the classroom, we must create a balance between our personal and professional lives. This is a challenge for us. We tend to treat them separately and often put so much time and energy into our teaching careers that our personal lives get shortchanged. Teachers have told me how they spend Sunday afternoons in their classroom while the rest of the family goes to a museum together; how they are too tired at the end of the day to read a novel; how they spend so much of their own money on books for their classroom that they can't afford to take a yoga course. They know that when they take time for their personal life, they are more centered in their professional life. However, the worries and stresses of teaching take over, and spending more and more time on teaching is an obvious and immediate response.

When I took special time with my family, I remember going to sleep that night with a deep sense of satisfaction. An extra hour of classroom planning didn't compare to a trip to the nature center or a family monopoly game, in terms of well-being for me and for my family. Having dinner with a friend restored my spirit and gave long-term benefits that another couple of hours creating a bulletin board could never give me.

Taking Time for Family and Friends

- List some ways that you balance your personal and professional life.
- List some areas that you need more balance between your personal and professional life.

Spending time with positive people

Spending time with positive people helps me center. Positive people encourage me to tap into the joys of life, inspire me to bring peace to myself and others, and affirm my desire to balance my personal and professional life. Thus, it is essential to do everything to keep my experiences positive.

At a personal level I choose friends who like to have fun, who find value in what they do, who appreciate the small as well as the big things in life, and who find humor as they go along. Whenever possible I try not to spend time with people who complain and never want solutions, who view life negatively, and who are afraid of new situations. On a professional level, I engage in conversations with educators who trust children, who want to find answers that benefit kids, and who love their job. I try to avoid those who talk about what kids can't do, who don't engage joyfully with children, who don't feel hopeful about children and the future of education, and who don't take their jobs seriously.

This doesn't mean that my friends and I don't have worries or that specific situations are problem free. But it does mean that we are willing to work for resolutions to various circumstances and that we trust we can find them. This also doesn't mean that I'm unwilling to help people who feel negative. But it does mean that I try to help them feel positive about possible solutions. In the course of a school day we find ourselves in many positive situations, as well as potentially negative circumstances that we can turn to positive experiences.

For example, before school the teacher across the hall shows me a successful project that a fourth grader has completed, and consequently, as the day starts, I celebrate the drawing by one of my first graders. Later at lunch, however, a few teachers complain about the negative behavior of their students. At this moment there are several ways I can respond. If I can't get centered, I might join the conversation and then feel worried and stressed about "the way kids are these days" without working toward a solution to the issue. I could tell the teachers to stop complaining, but that doesn't improve school morale or change attitudes, and it definitely doesn't center me. If I can think of my nuggets of truth, I have a better chance of remaining centered by ignoring the comments, by changing the conversation and saying something positive, or by leaving the room. Perhaps, also, I will be able to consider some long-range responses that can change the negative climate in the teachers' room and support the school staff in centering.

Spending Time with Positive People

- List five or more positive people with whom you spend time and tell what you do with them.
- List five positive-thinking people with whom you would like to spend time and describe what you'd like to do with them.
- List five negative situations that you would either like to eliminate in your life or to respond to positively. Tell how you can do this.

Being aware of what I am doing

I notice that I have more joy, peace, and balance when I am aware of what I'm doing and conscious of how I am reacting to various situations. This takes a great deal of practice and I find that when I slow down and even stop what I'm doing for a moment I have a better chance of centering and then responding proactively. I try to remember Hugh Prather's strategy at stressful moments *to stop, count to ten, think peace, and act with assurance.* Specifically, slowing down helps me study the situation and work for resolution, rather than react solely on a personal emotional level. It enables me to respond positively to potentially worrisome situations, and listen with empathy to another point of view.

During morning workshop one day in my classroom, I found myself worrying about the noise and physical activity in the classroom. My immediate reaction was to ring the bell and ask everyone to sit down and work silently. In other words, I wanted to cease my worrying by halting the outward behavior as expediently as possible. Instead, I stopped to listen and watch. What really was going on here? What was the nature of the noise? What was the nature of the activity? I noticed that as a group of children pored over a book about ancient Egypt, there was not enough room for everyone to see. I noticed that two children in the block area were working out the details of their building and hadn't yet come to an agreement. I noticed that the four children in the art area were laughing and talking about something, perhaps their projects.

Then I chose an immediate response. I spent a minute finding out what was interesting in the Egyptian book and then gave the group some other books to look at. I asked the block builders if they needed my help to work out their differences. They said no, but this little interlude seemed to settle them down and they returned to their conversation more calmly. I sat at the art table and helped the children refocus on their projects. By then I was able to decide upon my long-term response, which in this case was to discuss the escalating noise and activity before the next workshop.

Personal Guidelines for Responding to Classroom Situations

1. Observe the situation. Watch and listen to what is going on.
2. Observe myself. How am I feeling? What is my immediate reaction?
3. Observe the children. How are they reacting to the situation? How are they responding to each other?

4. Choose an appropriate immediate response.
5. Choose a suitable long-term response.
6. Note any reasons for my initial worry for later consideration.

I find that keeping aware of what I am doing and how I am reacting to various situations is an especially challenging aspect of centering. It takes practice to recall my positive strategies. This practice in responding positively to small stressful situations helps me when larger issues arise.

Being Aware of What I'm Doing

- Write about a time when you were not aware of your immediate response to a worrisome incident. What were the consequences? What would you have done differently had you watched and listened before reacting?
- Write about a time when you *did* watch and listen before responding. What did you learn from that situation?
- List some worrisome situations, of which you would like to improve your awareness.
- List some worrisome situations, to which you usually respond with awareness.

Accepting that everything in life is constantly changing

It is easier for me to stay centered when I expect and welcome change, since change is inevitable. As teachers, for example, we notice that the children grow and change physically, that they continually learn more and more about literacy, that the political issues in the field come and go in different forms, that new teachers and administrators work in our school, and that over the years we change some of our teaching strategies. In our personal life we observe the changing seasons, we see our own children getting bigger and our parents getting older, and we develop new hobbies and interests.

We embrace these big changes as part of life's process, whereas the small changes, which upon reflection seem insignificant and trivial, are often the hardest to accept and are apt to disrupt our centering most easily. At school we can't find the book we were planning to read to the class, a bus is late on the afternoon that we have bus duty, we were planning to write a few report cards when a parent stops by to talk. At home it's time for dinner and we've run out of milk, our daughter needs poster board for a school project due tomorrow, someone needs to get into the church and you're the only one he can find at home who has a key.

When I notice that I am not centered, I often observe that I am resisting the reality that some change that has taken place. I want things to be as they were, and so I talk and act as if the change had not occurred. Since this denial usually takes the form of complaining, I have to find someone who is willing to wallow in talk about how much better it was "in the good old days" The conversation stays unproductive as long as neither of us is willing to look at how we can benefit from the change. But as soon as I recall my rule to surround myself with positive people, my attitude concerning change begins to shift and I become more centered. My immediate options are either to refocus or terminate the conversation.

Accepting change has many implications for both our teaching and personal lives. When we expect change, we stop typecasting people and begin treating them in ways that give them the opportunity to develop and expand their abilities and interests. We see them with their complexities, ambiguities, and potential. We open up possibilities for our teaching and for the student's learning. Consider how the following comments can limit growth: *he's a follower; she isn't very social; she's a low group student; she's brilliant; he is always "good" in school.* When we expect change we give hope to the child struggling with reading, to the homeless, to the sick and the poor, to improving rundown schools, to students tempted by drugs.

Accepting Life's Changing Patterns

- Write about a time when you denied that a change had taken place. What were the consequences? What would you have done differently had you accepted the change?
- Write about a time when you had to accept a difficult change. What were the positive results? What results

were/are hard to accept? Are there any changes that
you still want to make in order to stay centered?
- List some changes that you are struggling to accept
and view positively.
- List some changes that you want to initiate.

Keeping a sense of humor

Teachers take their jobs extremely seriously, for they are held responsible for much of the intellectual, social, emotional, and physical growth of their students. Elementary teachers are entrusted with the same children six hours a day for one-hundred-eighty days a year. Middle and high school teachers have a much more limited time to support their students. Teacher educators have a tremendous responsibility in molding the future of education. Fortunately, successful teachers also have an inspiring sense of humor, which they call upon as one of the quickest ways to find their center and regain their balance.

Humor, as part of the curriculum, can be one of easiest ways to achieve academic goals and relieve stress at the same time. Some reluctant readers will read a joke to the class if given the opportunity and will accomplish a great deal of reading to find just the right joke. Children with "nothing to write about" will ease into writing by creating a joke book for the class, and learn about the question mark as they go along. Reading a humorous story to the class each day should be a staple of any read aloud program.

I must admit that when I was teaching I didn't always take full advantage of humor. I think I was afraid that I'd lose control, that the children would go into "fits of laughter," and that I couldn't get their attention back. But this wasn't always the case as long as I was laughing and letting my tension out right along with them. I wish I had been more relaxed about the four silly boys in my class one year. Even though I might never have understood their humor, I think I could have capitalized on their natural inclination and at least incorporated more silly songs and stories into the curriculum.

We also need to keep a sense of humor about ourselves and not treat ourselves too seriously. To be able to laugh at a mistake and share the humor with the class relaxes everyone and frees the children to accept their own mistakes. Showing our humanness, imperfections and all, allows our students to accept theirs as well. I can still picture Kristi raising her hand in group after we had returned from a field trip to the supermarket, and asking, "Mrs. Fisher, why do you have two different shoes on?" I just laughed and said that I hadn't noticed and that it hadn't affected the good time I had. Telling about funny incidents (such as the time we took a bag of garbage with us to Connecticut thinking it was a bag of Christmas presents) in our personal life helps maintain balance and gain mutual respect and trust.

Humor isn't just for the classroom, of course, but for our personal lives as well. Just as we can humor our student along, we can also apply humor to our personal lives. When we are feeling that we have too much to do, or that there are too many demands made on us by too many people, we can stop and realize that perhaps we are taking ourselves too seriously.

Keeping a Sense of Humor

- Where does humor exist in your curriculum? Where could you add more?
- Where does humor exist in your school day? Where could you add more?
- Where does humor exist in your personal life? Where could you add more?
- Write about three humorous incidents about yourself that you can tell your class.

Being open to spirituality

When I stay open to my own sense of spirituality, my personal and professional life becomes more centered and balanced. This takes continual and conscious effort, however. For me, being centered and balanced is a spiritual act, and I take seriously my commitment to keep this sense of awe at the forefront of what I do. I try to spend time every day praying and focusing on my faith; I continually examine my core religious beliefs so that they will become part of my everyday actions; and I keep my personal mission statement (see Chapter 11) at the forefront of the decisions I make.

Finding Our Spiritual Beliefs

Many teachers consider teaching a spiritual act. They teach because they want to touch the hearts of their students and make a difference in their lives. They lead their personal lives with the same spiritual commitment. As Parker Palmer, well-known writer and teacher, tells us, "Good teaching comes from the identity and integrity of the teacher" (1998, 10), to which I would add spirituality.

I believe that we hold beliefs about human beings and that these truths guide our actions both inside and outside the classroom. These may be clearly articulated theological presuppositions or subtle principles that subliminally run our lives. They have some commonalities with "nuggets of truth" in that both guide our actions and responses. Unlike "nuggets of truth," however, which guide our social actions, spiritual truths guide our intentions behind these actions. When we are able to articulate what we believe about humankind, we are better able to make decisions that support us in being centered and balanced. We can say yes or no in a difficult or controversial situation, and feel that our integrity has not been compromised and that perhaps it has even been strengthened.

Over the years, I have tried to apply the following spiritual truths in my work with children and teachers. I'm not always successful, but the more conscious I am of what I believe about human beings, the greater the possibility that these beliefs will be the foundation of my decisions and actions. A course I took with Brita Gill-Austern at Andover Newton Theological School helped me formulate and articulate some of these beliefs.

My purpose isn't to propose any particular religious tradition, ritual, or inclination but to provide some structures that teachers can use to define their own beliefs. For some this may include a particular religious tradition, and for others it may encompass a more general feeling of unity and love for the universe and humankind.

Human beings are made in the likeness of God

This spiritual truth presupposes that first and foremost we welcome everyone into our heart as an equal and that we don't favor one person over another. We try to meet all people at their point of holiness, without regard to the obvious characteristics of race, class, gender, age, and physical appearance; the more transparent characteristics such as education, health, political beliefs, talent, and sexual orientation; or the psychological themes in our lives, such as confidence or rejection, abundance or loss, health or illness, blithe or melancholy, and freedom or addictions. This perspective helps us advocate for children and policies, as well as steer away from favoritism and personal power.

Human beings are continually changing

When we view human beings as forever changing, we stop categorizing or judging them according to what they were in the past or what they are now. Thinking of life as journey allows for transformation, and opens up the possibility for us to change bad habits, addictions, prejudices, and negative life themes, and to grow toward compassion, justice, and empowerment. As we continue on the journey, we build on what has come before and create new ways of being in the future. Although the events in our lives effect our growth, we also have the capacity within us to influence this growth. This truth helps us treat students with hope: the insecure child can gain confidence and the struggling reader can learn to read. It gives us the hope for societal and political transformation and the belief that the individual student or teacher is also capable of changing.

Human beings constantly search for meaning

Whether consciously or unconsciously, we are always searching for meaning, and when we feel that our lives lack meaning, we take action and try something new that will satisfy us. Viktor Frankl, theologian and writer during the holocaust, wrote that the primary motivational factor in a person's life is the search for meaning and that we discover meaning by: (1) creating a work or doing a deed; (2) experiencing something or encountering someone; and (3) the attitude we take toward unavoidable suffering (1984, 133). When there is meaning in our lives, we are more apt to feel purposeful in our work and at peace with our family and friends. This doesn't mean that we are without problems, sadness, or even suffering, but it does imply that we aren't bored, aimless, or melancholy, and that we are able to take positive action. This truth reminds us that our students are also searching for meaning and that they need challenges that are meaningful, interesting, and purposeful to them.

Human beings are unique and independent individuals

Each human being is a unique individual, with a unique disposition, temperament, culture, and life history. When we reflect on the individuality and uniqueness of human beings, we are drawn into the mystery of life. In a crowd we can be overwhelmed by an awareness that *all those people* are individuals, with an ever-evolving custom-made itinerary for their life's journey, which in many respects will forever remain a mystery to us. This gives us tremendous respect for our students. Only in the most general terms do we know what they might need to learn. They need to tell us how they learn and what their true interests and passions are.

Human beings are connected to others

Human beings also long to be included and connected to others. We are social beings, unable to move through life alone. How we relate to others has direct bearing on ourselves as individuals. Frankl tells us that, "Our survival and development depends on our capacity to recruit the invested attention of others to us" (17). Others reflect who we are as individuals by including us, praising us, ignoring us, or responding negatively to us. We need others to help us successfully construct our life work, for whatever we do, either individually or collectively, almost always involves experiencing something or encountering someone. Frankl goes on to suggest that "love is the only way to grasp another human being in the innermost core of his personality" (134). This suggests that we must reach out to a wider social community than our immediate classroom, school system, family, or social network. It means working toward the integration of a just society for all. It means not only feeling compassion but working for justice.

Finding Our Spiritual Truths

Write your spiritual truths. You might want to start with a long list and then go back and revise and consolidate. It may help clarify your truths if you write about each one during the listing process.

11

Writing a Mission Statement and Taking Time for Ourselves

LIKE THE other chapters in Part Two of this book, the two sections in this chapter draw from teacher workshops that I have given. They originate from my belief that when we think through and write a professional mission statement, and when we take time for personal reflection, exercise, hobbies, and interests, we maintain balance and stay centered.

Writing a Mission Statement

Many years ago I wrote a personal mission statement for a course I was taking. It went something like this: *My mission is to bring happiness to myself and others.* Over the years I have revised it to its present form. For example, the verb *to bring*, written in the passive voice, doesn't actively or specifically describe what I want to do, which is to *inspire, affirm, and encourage. Happiness* as a goal seemed too trivial, so I changed it to *peace, joy, and balance.* Originally, I had put *myself* before *others* because I believed that in order to help others, I first had to take care of myself. There is some truth in that, but I now think of myself as walking the journey *with* others and that I don't always have to be happy in order to support someone else. This general mission statement has evolved into a professional mission statement, and consequently I have omitted myself from the statement: *My mission is to inspire, affirm, and encourage peace, joy, and balance in teachers.*

The mission statement has three parts:

1. active verbs that describe what I do
2. dynamic nouns that describe the goals I want
3. a proper noun that names who I want to work with, called my *focus*

The creation of my mission statement involved four steps, which are described below.

Step 1

Step one involved deciding with whom I wanted to work, since I had recently retired from the classroom and I wasn't certain what my new work would be. Did I want to work with children? Did I want to continue to work with teachers, or did I want to focus on another sector of society, such as those in the last period of their lives whom I visited as a hospice volunteer? Were there other possibilities that I had never considered? I spent a great deal of time thinking and writing about this because I was aware that if I didn't get a clear vision of whom I wanted to work with, I would find myself bouncing about, doing a little of this and a little of that, without a sense of accomplishment.

Step 2

After deciding that I wanted to continue the major part of my work with teachers, I concentrated on step two, examining what to do. I asked myself two questions: What to I *want* to do? What *are* my talents and inclinations? These questions are related but distinct, for often I want to do something that I'm just not very good at, and sometimes there are things that I can do but that don't interest me. Since this mission statement was going to guide my decisions for the next ten years or so, I wanted to be as clear, honest, and precise as possible with my choice of words.

As I started describing what I wanted to do, I found *The Path: Creating Your Mission Statement for Work and for Life* by Laurie Beth Jones most helpful, especially the alphabetical list of more than one-hundred-seventy verbs to choose from to define what I wanted to do. I settled on the three that most clearly represented what I *could* do and what I *wanted* to do for teachers. This took several days of listing, reviewing, crossing out, adding, and rearranging before I settled on *inspire, affirm, and encourage*, which define and uphold my trust in teachers to make their own decisions.

Step 3

The third step involved choosing goals that would speak to all teachers. I chose *peace, joy, and balance,* because regardless of life experiences and circumstances, I believe that all teachers are searching for these goals.

Step 4

After completing my mission statement, I realized that although I wrote it for professional purposes, the goals and actions that I selected could work equally well if I changed the focus and substituted *family and friends,* or *humankind.* When our mission statement honestly represents what we can do and what we value, we can apply it to other life situations.

Writing a Mission Statement

Start by writing a few mission statements as part of a freewrite, and then settle on a first draft.

- Step 1: Name Your Focus.

Although the audience of your mission is listed last in the statement, I suggest that you name it first. For teachers, the focus will probably be your students. You might want to specifically name the students: elementary, middle, high school, inservice, or graduate, depending on your area of focus.

- Step 2: Describe What You Do.

This part of the mission statement takes the most time and effort. Begin by generating a list of verbs. Write down every one that comes to your mind. You might want to take some breaks and return to the list at a later time.

Over time, settle on three verbs that best represent what you want to do and what you can do. Write the verbs in the order that you want them to appear in your mission statement.

- Step 3: Describe Your Goals.

To choose your goals, follow the same steps described in Step 2. Begin by generating a list of goals for your focus. Write down each idea that comes to your mind. Again, you might want to take some breaks and return to the list at a later time.

Over time, settle on three goals that best represent what you want to help your focus achieve. Write them in the order that you want them to appear in your mission statement.

- Step 4: Write Your Mission Statement.

Taking Time for Ourselves

One of the main themes of this book is that we need time if we want to balance our personal and professional lives and stay centered. And yet, through face-to-face conversations and e-mail correspondence, teachers again and again tell me how difficult it is for them to take time for themselves. They are too busy, and when they do take time they feel guilty because they know they could be doing more for school, or spending time with family or friends. They agree, however, that when they do take some personal time, they are better teachers, friends, and family members. Their bodies relax, their minds shift from the daily responsibilities, and they feel they have some personal control over their lives.

Getting started

How do we give ourselves permission to take time for ourselves? How do we carve out a little time each day when we feel we don't have time? I believe that we will only do this when we truly believe that we deserve it for our own well-being and piece of mind, when we stop feeling guilty about enjoying fifteen minutes reading, taking a bubble bath, walking in the woods, exercising, or sitting in silence. In workshops teachers tell me how difficult it is for them to give themselves permission to do this, so I tell them that until they can stop feeling guilty and give themselves permission, I will give it to them. They leave promising themselves fifteen minutes of "free" time every day for a week.

Taking Time for Ourselves

- List three different times in the day when you might be able to give fifteen minutes to yourself (early morning, at lunchtime, immediately when you get home from school, after dinner when the family is doing the dishes, when everyone else has gone to bed). Put an asterisk next to the one that seems most possible.
- Brainstorm a list of everything you would like to do during this time. At this point don't consider how long something might take (carpentry, folk dance, lift weights, listen to music, meditate, paint, read, ski, walk, write poetry). Narrow the list to three things that you could do in the fifteen-minute time period you selected. Put an asterisk next to the one you'll start with tomorrow. Be sure to keep the list for future use and add to it when a new idea comes to mind.
- Give yourself permission for a week (or take permission from me) do what you have chosen. You might want to keep a journal about when you've done and how you've felt about it. How has this daily fifteen minutes enhanced the balance in your life? Has it upset the balance in any way, and what can you do about that? Do you feel more centered?

Once we get into the routine and feel the freedom of having personal time, we can begin to adjust it to our particular schedule. There is nothing sacred about fifteen minutes, in fact it is not enough time in most cases but it gets the habit going. Some teachers take fifteen minutes at the beginning and end of the day, others find that on certain days it is impossible even to steal a minute from their busy schedule. Others spend more time on the weekend and added time on vacations. Our ultimate goal is to take time on a regular basis for quiet reading and reflection, exercise, and interests and hobbies.

Taking time for reflection

I believe that it is essential that we take time for reflection if we want maintain a sense of balance in our personal and professional lives and remain centered. We need time to consider our "nuggets of truth" and how they apply to our everyday lives. We need time to reach deeply into our spiritual place for answers that we can't get through our everyday living. We need time to let our minds rest and be still. For some, this involves participating in a particular religious tradition, whereas for others it entails creating their own spiritual practices and understandings. This daily solitude becomes the springboard from which we take time for ourselves in other areas of our lives.

Taking Time for Reflection

- Take a moment to write about the spiritual or religious tradition that supports you at this time in your life.
- What reflection practices support you? Prayer? Meditation? Spiritual readings?
- What books or readings might support you in this practice?
- When in the day is the best reflection time for you?
- Where can you find quiet and solitude for reflection?
- What new ideas, institutions, readings, or reflection practices do you want to explore?

Taking time for exercise

It is generally agreed that daily exercise is essential for a healthy mind and body. This includes walking, jogging, working out in a gym, aerobics, yoga, and swimming, all of which usually take more than fifteen minutes and often call for special equipment, clothing, and preparation. Teachers who build exercise into their daily routine report that they feel better, respond more positively to their students and family, and are better able to balance their personal and professional lives and to stay centered.

Taking Time for Exercise

- What is your present daily exercise schedule?
- What would you like to do differently?
- Choose an exercise plan that you can begin within the next week.

Taking time for hobbies

Teachers long to pursue their own interests and hobbies beyond the confines of what they teach. As they heed Joseph Campbell's call and follow their bliss, their life takes on balance. When they learn a craft, play a musical instrument, sing in a choir, take a calligraphy course, read about a favorite period in history, go away on a personal retreat or trip, or write a novel, they feel spiritually enriched and centered.

Taking Time for Interests and Hobbies

Return to the original brainstorming list of things you like to do that you started in "Creating a Personal Inventory" (page 113). Add to the list. Be creative and adventuresome, adding ideas that don't seem possible or probable to you. Group the possibilities in to the following categories.

> Collections (e.g., antiques)
> Crafts (quilting)
> Joining a group (local orchestra)
> Projects (refinishing the kitchen)
> Sports (mountain climbing)
> Study topics (Inca civilization)
> Travel (cruise around Greece)

Put an asterisk next to the one in each category that you want to do most, or that you think is possible to start. Pick one and begin this weekend.

Teachers know that in order to stay centered and balanced they need to follow their personal beliefs and stay committed to their life's mission. Finding the time to think deeply about these spiritual aspects is their biggest challenge and most important task. When we do take time for ourselves, we are a better friend and family member, and a more joyful teacher.

JOYS of teaching include . . . when my young learners emulate me, and role play being the teacher. . . . When we laugh together. . . . When we sing nonsense rhyming and repetitive songs with the accompaniment of my guitar. . . . When they plead for me to "Read that story again!" . . . When they come up to me and say, "I can read this!" . . . When we have established trust and acceptance within our community of learners, and everyone demonstrates a sharing and caring attitude for one another. . . . When I'm feeling frantic inside ('cause I wish I had more parent helpers) while trying to meet everyone's needs, and a student asks me to load a different program on our computer and it takes me forever to locate it and get back to her . . . and when I do, I apologize for the delay and she replies, "That's okay Mrs. C., I didn't grow old yet." The joys are infinite; they always seem to outweigh the stresses.

E-mail from a kindergarten teacher

APPENDIX
E-mail Letters to Teachers

Letter 1

BEFJoyful@aol.com
February 15, 1999

Dear Teacher Friend,

For the past several years I have been working with classroom teachers throughout the country. They have often mentioned to me that although teaching is an extremely rewarding profession, in their experience it is also very demanding and stressful. Many have said that they were interested in hearing about the various ways that other teachers balance their personal and professional lives.

In this regard, I have recently begun research for a book for teachers that will address this topic, and I would very much appreciate receiving your thoughts on how you stay centered and maintain your peace of mind both inside and outside the classroom. I will keep any comments you share with me strictly confidential, of course, and I will not use your name without your written permission.

I am especially interested in any of your thoughts on the following issues. It would also be helpful if you would indicate your teaching location, grade level and/or position. You may e-mail me at BEFJoyful@aol.com.

- What are some of the specific stresses in your teaching situation and how do you deal with them?
- When are the times that you feel the most joy in your teaching?
- How do you help your students deal with stress?

- What are some of the stresses in your personal life that affect your teaching and how do you deal with them?
- What interests and hobbies help you stay balanced?
- Do you have a religious or spiritual orientation that helps you deal with stress?
- Are there persons in your life who have served as role models?
- What books and articles have helped you personally and professionally?

I am hoping to reach a large number of teachers with this letter, and I would appreciate it if you would e-mail or give copies of it to any of your colleagues who might like to respond. I hope the year is going well for you, and thanks for your help.

Best wishes,

Bobbi Fisher

Letter 2

BEFJoyful@aol.com
March 9, 1999

Dear Teacher Friend,

A great big *Thank-you* to those of you who responded to my letter. Your stories about the ways that you deal with stress, balance your personal and professional lives, and stay centered are invaluable for the book I am writing for teachers on that subject. So far, I have received more than seventy e-mail responses from elementary, middle and secondary teachers, curriculum coordinators, and college teachers in twenty-five states, as well as Canada and South America, with more coming in every day.

Many teachers answered the question, "When are the times that you feel the most joy in your teaching?" by telling stories of both their delight, and that of their students, when learning occurs. Other professional joys involved supportive colleagues, administrators, and parents. Some of their professional stresses were caused by state standards, testing, the difficulty of meeting the special needs of children when no professional help is available, unsympathetic administrators, and demanding or indifferent parents. Teachers also related many ways that they overcome difficulties and turn negative situations into productive possibilities. They help their students deal with stress by listening to them, reading stories, holding class meetings, planning relaxing moments in class, and providing comfortable places in the classroom.

Family and friends were essential for most teachers' well-being, although many said that their children, parents, and spouses take a great deal of their time, leaving very little time for themselves. To relieve stress they try to find time to pray, exercise, talk with friends, listen to music, and pursue hobbies. A specific religious faith was especially helpful to some, and a good number said that although they were not affiliated with a particular faith, they prayed a lot during difficult situations. Many admitted that they give more time to their job than to their family, and that they feel guilty about it. Role models included spouses, parents, grandparents, principals, church figures, and authors. They read professional and inspirational books, novels, and children's literature to help them relax.

In the book I am planning to use the words *centering* and *balancing* to describe what teachers are striving for. Although many of you gave examples of times when you felt centered or balanced, it is apparent that these words mean different things to different people. For example, some think of being centered as living with intensity, while others feel centered when they are calm. Thus I would appreciate your thoughts on the following questions:

- What does being centered mean to you and how do you know when you are centered?
- What does being balanced mean to you and how do you know when you are balanced?
- Does being centered and being balanced mean the same to you?

I hope that you will continue to send my letters out to colleagues. I will keep any comments strictly confidential, and will not use names without written permission. Thanks for your help.

Best wishes,

Bobbi Fisher

Letter 3

BEFJoyful@aol.com
April 8, 1999

Dear Teacher Friends,

Many of you have responded to my previous letters asking about ways that you balance your personal and professional lives. Thank you for your thoughtful messages.

Many of the e-mails I received mentioned state standards and testing as a major obstacle to teaching and learning. Your responses to the following questions would be very helpful.

- How do state standards and testing create stress for you and how do you handle it?
- How do state standards and testing create stress for your students and how do you help them handle it?
- What are some alternatives to standards and testing that would help your students' learning?

Also, in my book I plan to include your suggestions concerning the ways administrators and parents can help to alleviate stress in the classroom. I would appreciate your thoughts on the following questions:

- What can parents do to help you with your job?
- What can administrators do to create a positive school atmosphere and help you as a teacher?
- What can be done to reduce the nonteaching tasks and increasing curriculum demands that take away from your planning and teaching time?

I hope that you will continue to send my letters out to colleagues. I will keep any comments strictly confidential, and will not use names without written permission. It would also be helpful if you would indicate your teaching location, grade level and/or position. You may e-mail me at BEFJoyful@aol.com.

Thanks for your help.

Best wishes,

Bobbi Fisher

P.S. For those of you hearing about my project for the first time, let me briefly explain. I have recently begun writing for a book for teachers that will address the various ways that teachers deal with stress and balance their personal and professional lives. I would be pleased to receive your thoughts on this general topic. If you would like a copy of the original questions, please e-mail me and I will send them to you.

Letter 4

BEFJoyful@aol.com
April 22, 1999

Dear Teacher Friend,

I am writing to you in the midst of the sorrow we all are experiencing over the tragedy in Littleton, Colorado.

For the past two and a half months I have been in correspondence with many of you about the stresses in your lives and how you stay centered and balance your personal and professional lives. Almost all of you have written that in order for teaching and learning to happen in your classrooms, you and the students must create a caring, stress-free environment. Those who work day in and day out with students know that self-esteem, socializing, and rigorous learning cannot be separated.

At this sorrowful time I believe that teachers are one of the best hopes for healing, and that they can make a difference by continuing to speak out about the importance of supporting and maintaining a climate of care and concern in their classrooms and schools.

With love,

Bobbi Fisher

Letter 5

BEFJoyful@aol.com
June 11, 1999

Dear Teacher Friend,

Many of you have answered the previous letters that I sent asking about the various ways that you deal with the stresses in your lives. I have greatly appreciated your answers to my questions, and hope that you will continue to e-mail me if you think of anything to add. As you know, your responses are contributing to a book I am writing about ways teachers balance their personal and professional lives.

In my book I plan to include a chapter about purpose and life goals and how they help teachers deal successfully with the stresses in their lives. I would very much value your thoughts on this topic, including, if relevant, your own personal mission statement, calling, vocation, and/or life purpose.

Many of you have started that much-needed summer vacation, and some of you will be celebrating that last day of school soon. I hope that every one of you is able to find time to rest and get away for a change of pace, and to pursue a personal interest. You'll know you're on vacation when you wake up one morning and realize that you have slept through the night.

Best wishes,

Bobbi Fisher

Letter 6

BEFJoyful@aol.com
July 26, 1999

Dear Teacher Friend,

Many of you have received letters from me asking you to respond to various questions about how you deal with stress and balance your personal and professional lives. Your responses have been most helpful for the book I am writing on this subject.

In many of those responses, certain topics have come up that are specific to the particular circumstances of individual teachers. If any of the following topics are pertinent to your situation, I would appreciate hearing your stories and the ways that you cope with the stresses involved:

- parenting your own parents
- health issues
- financial concerns

- handling divorce
- single parenting
- living and being alone
- gay and lesbian issues

I am also writing a chapter pertaining to first-year teachers and would like to hear about the joys and stresses of that first year. How did you "get through" the year? What suggestions do you have for teachers just beginning their careers? What can school systems, administrators and "seasoned" teachers do to help first-year teachers?

Please feel free to share this letter with friends. I will keep any comments you share with me strictly confidential, of course, and I will not use your name without your written permission.

Hope you are enjoying your much-deserved summer vacation.

Best wishes,

Bobbi Fisher

Letter 7

BEFJoyful@aol.com
September 30, 1999

Dear Teacher Friend,

Many of you have received some or all of my previous letters asking you to respond to questions about how you deal with stress. For those of you hearing from me for the first time, I am writing a book about how teachers balance their personal and professional lives and stay centered.

As I continue to write, new topics arise that I believe are important to address in the book. If any of the following seem pertinent to your situation, I would appreciate hearing from you about them and the ways that you cope with the stresses involved:

- divorce
- single parenting
- living and being alone
- gay and lesbian issues
- first year of teaching

I am also interested in responses to the following questions:

- How do your own childhood experiences affect your vocation as a teacher?
- How does your ethnic and/or cultural situation affect your teaching?

Finally, I would like to include comments from teachers about how their spiritual tradition supports their teaching.

Please feel free to share this letter with friends. I will keep any comments you send me strictly confidential, of course, and I will not use your name without your written permission.

Best wishes,

Bobbi Fisher

Letter 8

BEFJoyful@aol.com
January 4, 2000

Dear Teacher Friend,

Many of you have received some or all of my previous letters asking you to respond to questions about how you deal with stress. For those of you hearing from me for the first time, I am writing a book about how teachers balance their personal and professional lives and stay centered.

Presently I am writing a chapter addressing how state/school system standards and testing influence teachers and students. I would like to receive comments to any or all of the following questions. Those of you who have already written to me about this topic, please feel free to add to any new thoughts.

- Do the standards and tests represent what your students know and have learned?
- Are they developmentally appropriate for your students?
- Do they support your curriculum?
- Are you able to use the testing results for diagnostic purposes?

- In regard to your school system's economic position, has testing influenced you and your students?
- Do you see any equity issues that need to be addressed?
- Has the emphasis on standards and testing either undermined or supported your professionalism?
- Have the parents of your students responded or reacted to testing?
- Have you spoken up publicly about standards and testing?

Please share this letter with friends. I will keep any comments you send me strictly confidential, of course. Although I plan to include quotes from teachers in my book, I will not use your name without your written permission.

Best wishes,

Bobbi Fisher

TEACHERS' READING LIST

This list contains books and websites that teachers mentioned in response to my e-mail question, "What books and articles have helped you personally and professionally?" I have also included some of my favorites.

Finding Personal Balance

Albom, Mitch. 1997. *Tuesdays with Morrie*. New York: Doubleday.

Belenky, Mary Field. 1987, 1997. *Women's Ways of Knowing: The Development of Self, Voice, and Mind*. New York: Basic Books.

The Bible

Bly, Carol. 1996. *Changing the Bully Who Rules the World: Reading and Thinking About Ethics*. Minneapolis: Milkweed Editions.

Breathnach, Sarah Ban. 1995. *Simple Abundance: A Daybook of Comfort and Joy*. New York: Warner Books.

Buber, Martin. 1996. *I and Thou*. New York: Touchstone Books.

Cameron, Julia. 1992. *The Artist's Way: A Spiritual Path to Higher Creativity*. New York: G. P. Putnam.

Campbell, Joseph. 1973. *The Hero with a Thousand Faces*. Princeton: Princeton University Press.

Carlson, Richard, and Joseph Bailey. 1998. *Slowing Down to the Speed of Life: How to Create a More Peaceful, Simpler Life from the Inside Out*. San Francisco: HarperCollins.

Copeland, Mary Ellen. 1998. *The Worry Control Workbook*. Oakland, CA: New Harbinger Publications.

Covey, Stephen. 1989. *The Seven Habits of Highly Effective People: Powerful Lessons in Personal Change*. New York: Simon & Schuster.

Edelman, Marian Wright. 1992. *The Measure of Our Success: A Letter to My Children and Yours*. Boston: Beacon Press.

Foster, Richard J. 1992. *Prayer: Finding the Heart's True Home*. San Francisco: HarperCollins.

Frankl, Viktor E. 1984. *Man's Search for Meaning*. New York: Washington Square Press.

Gire, Ken. 1998. *The Reflective Life: Becoming More Spiritually Sensitive to the Everyday Moments of Life*. Colorado Springs: Chariot Victor Publishing.

Glanz, Jeffrey. 2000. *Relax for Success: An Educator's Guide to Stress Management*. Norwood, MA: Christopher-Gordon.

Jones, Laurie Beth. 1996. *The Path: Creating Your Mission Statement for Work and for Life*. New York: Hyperion.

Kissen, Rita. 1996. *The Last Closet: The Real Lives of Lesbian and Gay Teachers*. Portsmouth, NH: Heinemann.

Lamott, Anne. 1999. *Traveling Mercies: Some Thoughts on Faith*. New York: Pantheon Books.

Lehmkuhl, Dorothy, and Dolores Lamping. 1993. *Organizing for the Creative Person*. New York: Three Rivers Press.

Lindbergh, Anne Morrow. [1955] 1991. *Gift from the Sea*. New York: Random House.

Prather, Hugh. 1986. *Notes on How to Live in the World . . . and Still Be Happy*. New York: Doubleday.

Rinpoche, Sogyal. 1992. *The Tibetan Book of Living and Dying*. San Francisco: HarperCollins.

Surya Das, Lama. 1997. *Awakening the Buddha Within: Tibetan Wisdom for the Western World*. New York: Broadway Books.

Woolf, Virginia. [1929] 1981. *A Room of One's Own*. New York: Harcourt Brace.

Finding Professional Balance

Atwell, Nancy. 1998. *In the Middle: New Understandings About Writing, Reading, and Learning*. 2d ed. Portsmouth, NH: Heinemann.

Avery, Carol. 1993. *. . . And with a Light Touch: Learning about Reading, Writing, and Teaching with First Graders*. Portsmouth, NH: Heinemann.

Burke, Jim. 1999a. *The English Teacher's Companion*. Portsmouth, NH: Heinemann.

————. 1999b. *I Hear America Reading: Why We Read, What We Read.* Portsmouth, NH: Heinemann.

Caine, Renate, and Geoffrey Caine. 1991. *Making Connections: Teaching and the Human Brain.* Alexandria, VA: Association for Supervision and Curriculum Development.

Calkins, Lucy. 1994. *The Art of Teaching Writing.* New ed. Portsmouth, NH: Heinemann.

————. 1998. *A Teacher's Guide to Standardized Reading Tests.* Portsmouth, NH: Heinemann.

Cambourne, Brian. 1988. *The Whole Story: Natural Learning and the Acquisition of Literacy in the Classroom.* New York: Scholastic.

Clay, Marie. 1991. *Becoming Literate: The Construction of Inner Control.* Portsmouth, NH: Heinemann.

————. 1993. *An Observation Survey of Early Literacy Achievement.* Portsmouth, NH: Heinemann.

Coles, Gerald. 2000. *Misreading Reading: The Bad Science That Hurts Children.* Portsmouth, NH: Heinemann.

Dewey, John. 1938, 1963. *Experience and Education.* New York: Macmillan.

Edelsky, Carol, Bess Altwerger, and Barbara Flores. 1990. *Whole Language: What's the Difference?* Portsmouth, NH: Heinemann.

Fisher, Bobbi. 1995. *Thinking and Learning Together: Curriculum and Community in a Primary Classroom.* Portsmouth, NH: Heinemann.

————. 1996. *Inside the Classroom: Teaching Kindergarten and First Grade.* Portsmouth, NH: Heinemann.

————. 1998. *Joyful Learning in Kindergarten.* Revised ed. Portsmouth, NH: Heinemann.

Fisher, Bobbi, and Emily Fisher Medvic. 2000. *Perspectives on Shared Reading: Planning and Practice.* Portsmouth, NH: Heinemann.

Fletcher, Ralph. 1993. *What a Writer Needs.* Portsmouth, NH: Heinemann.

Freire, Paulo. 1970, 1993. *Pedagogy of the Oppressed.* New York: Continuum Publishing Company.

Frye, Northrup. 1964. *The Educated Imagination.* Bloomington, IN: Indiana University Press.

Garcia, Cara. 1998. *Too Scared to Learn: Overcoming Academic Anxiety.* Thousand Oaks, CA: Corwin Press.

Gardner, Howard. 1993. *Creating Minds.* New York: Basic Books.

Glazer, Steven, ed. 1999. *The Heart of Learning: Spirituality in Education.* New York: Putnam.

Glover, Mary K. 1997. *Making School by Hand*. Urbana, IL: National Council of Teachers of English.

———. 1999. *A Garden of Poets*. Urbana, IL: National Council of Teachers of English.

Goleman, Daniel. 1995. *Emotional Intelligence: Why It Can Matter More Than IQ*. New York: Bantam.

Goodman, Kenneth. 1986. *What's Whole in Whole Language?* Portsmouth, NH: Heinemann.

———. 1998. *In Defense of Good Teaching: What Teachers Need to Know About the "Reading Wars."* York, ME: Stenhouse.

Graves, Donald. 1989. *Discover Your Own Literacy*. Portsmouth, NH: Heinemann.

———. 1994. *A Fresh Look at Writing*. Portsmouth, NH: Heinemann.

Harwayne, Shelley. 1999. *Going Public: Priorities and Practice at The Manhattan New School*. Portsmouth, NH: Heinemann.

Heard, Georgia. 1992. *For the Good of the Earth and Sun: Teaching Poetry*. Portsmouth, NH: Heinemann.

Holt, John. 1990 (reprinted edition). *Learning All the Time*. Cambridge, MA: Perseus Publishing.

Johnston, Peter. 1997. *Knowing Literacy: Constructive Literacy Assessment*. York, ME: Stenhouse.

Keene, Ellin, and Susan Zimmermann. 1997. *Mosaic of Thought: Teaching Comprehension in a Reader's Workshop*. Portsmouth, NH: Heinemann.

Kohn, Alfie. 1993. *Punished by Rewards: The Trouble with Gold Stars, Incentive Plans, As, Praise, and Other Bribes*. Boston: Houghton Mifflin.

Kozol, Jonathan. 1991. *Savage Inequalities: Children in America's Schools*. New York: Crown.

Levy, Steven. 1996. *Starting from Scratch: One Classroom Builds Its Own Curriculum*. Portsmouth, NH: Heinemann.

Mills, Heidi, Tim O'Keefe, amd Diane Stephens. 1992. *Looking Closely: Exploring the Role of Phonics in One Whole Language Classroom*. Urbana, IL: National Council of Teachers of English.

Murray, Donald. 1990. *Shoptalk: Learning to Write with Writers*. Portsmouth, NH: Boynton/Cook.

Neill, Alexander. 1995. *Summerhill School: A New View of Childhood*. Revised ed. New York: St. Martin's Press.

Noddings, Nel. 1992. *The Challenge to Care in Schools: An Alternative Approach to Education*. New York: Teachers College Press.

Ohanian, Susan. 1999. *One Size Fits Few: The Folly of Educational Standards.* Portsmouth, NH: Heinemann.

O'Reilley, Mary Rose. 1998. *Radical Presence: Teaching as Contemplative Practice.* Portsmouth, NH: Heineman.

Palmer, Parker J. 1998. *The Courage to Teach: Exploring the Inner Landscape of a Teacher's Life.* San Francisco: Jossey-Bass.

————. 1983, 1993. *To Know as We Are Known: Education as a Spiritual Journey.* San Francisco: Harper.

Pennac, Daniel. 1999. *Better than Life.* York, ME: Stenhouse.

Poplin, Mary, and Joseph Weeres. 1992. *Voices from the Inside: A Report on Schooling from Inside the Classroom.* Claremont, CA: The Institute for Education in Transformation at Claremont Graduate University.

Rief, Linda. 1992. *Seeking Diversity: Language Arts with Adolescents.* Portsmouth, NH: Heinemann.

Routman. Regie. 1994. *Invitations.* Portsmouth, NH: Heinemann.

————. 2000. *Conversations.* Portsmouth, NH: Heinemann

Short, Kathy, and Jerome Harste. 1996. *Creating Classrooms for Authors and Inquirers.* Portsmouth, NH: Heinemann.

Smith, Frank. 1995. *Between Hope and Havoc: Essays into Human Learning and Education.* Portsmouth, NH: Heinemann.

Taylor, Denny. 1991. *Learning Denied.* Portsmouth, NH: Heinemann.

Vygotsky, Lev S. 1968, 1978. *Mind in Society: The Development of Higher Psychological Processes.* Cambridge, MA: Harvard University Press.

Websites

CATENet is provided by the California Association of Teachers of English: *http://www.cateweb.org*.

Center for Teacher Formation: *http://www.Teacherformation.org*.

Fair Test: National Center for Fair and Open Testing: *http://www.fairtest.org*.

National Council of Teachers of English: *http://www.ncte.org*.

TAWL subscription page: *http://www.Wholelanguageumbrella*.

Teachers.Net: The Online Resource for Educators: *http://teachers.net*.